Anora

INT. HEADQUARTERS (MANHATTAN) - NIGHT

The night is banging at HEADQUARTERS, a gentlemen's club in the heart of the city. A large central part of the room is filled with couches and seats where flirting and light lap dances happen. Around the edge of that are smaller curtained off areas and rooms where even more "in-depth" dances and interactions happen. A pop song blasts in the club. There are 50 girls and 15 guys downstairs and 20 girls and 5 guys upstairs. Throughout the club are 3 security guards, a DJ, the owner and the owner's right hand man. The music is so loud that everyone is essentially shouting at all times.

The camera dollies down a row of lap dances, one after another. Some are heavy grinding while others are putting on a show. We land on the sixth dancer who is facing away from her customer as she thrusts back on him. This is ANI (23). The camera locks on a medium CU shot on her face.

The opening credits roll over this section.

                                           HARD CUT TO:

INT. HEADQUARTERS - VARIOUS - NIGHT - LATER

The camera follows Ani throughout her night, establishing the club's operations, social interactions, clientele and geography. It's full of private rooms each with their own style. Ani performs different types of dances, some private, some out in the open.

                                                CUT TO:

INT. HEADQUARTERS - FIRST FLOOR BAR - NIGHT - LATER

Ani sweet talks a BUSINESSMAN (50's) into getting a dance.

INT. HEADQUARTERS - FIRST FLOOR - NIGHT

Ani gives a lap dance to a client. There is casual small talk with the customer, keeping it light and fun.

INT. HEADQUARTERS - FIRST FLOOR - NIGHT

Ani gives a lap dance to a client in a different area.

INT. HEADQUARTERS - FIRST FLOOR - NIGHT

Ani gives a lap dance to a client in a different area.

INT. HEADQUARTERS - FIRST FLOOR - NIGHT

Ani gives a lap dance to a client in a different area.

OMITTED

INT. HEADQUARTERS - PRIVATE ROOM - NIGHT - LATER

She gives a topless lap dance to a DUDE (40) in a different private room.

CUT TO:

INT. HEADQUARTERS - PRIVATE ROOM - NIGHT - LATER

She gives a more performance-type lap dance to another DUDE (58) in a different private room.

OMITTED

INT. HEADQUARTERS - BACKSTAIRS - NIGHT - LATER

Ani's friend/co-worker LULU (19) walks down the stairs and scans the room. She sees Ani and motions to her - putting up two fingers and pointing upstairs. Ani sees this and excuses herself from the bar conversation she's having.

CUT TO:

OMITTED

INT. HEADQUARTERS - PRIVATE ROOM - NIGHT - LATER

Ani and Lulu give a private 2-on-1 dance to a middle aged man. While grinding, without the guy noticing, they exchange looks that say... "want to smoke?"

EXT. HEADQUARTERS - FRONT SIDEWALK - NIGHT - LATER

In the winter night, Ani and Lulu shiver as they pass a blunt back and forth. A bouncer is admitting two businessmen into the club in the background.

INT. HEADQUARTERS - MAIN FLOOR - NIGHT

From a distance, we observe Ani and her co-workers work the main floor. (We roll without a cut for ten minutes) Ani knows some of the clients by their first name.

Ani passes by DIAMOND (23). They clearly are not fond of each other.

                    DIAMOND
          Ani, was Robert at the club
          yesterday?

                    ANI
          Yeah.

                    DIAMOND
          And did he ask for a dance?

                    ANI
          Yeah.

                    DIAMOND
          And did you give him one?

                    ANI
          Yeah?

Diamond is not pleased.

                    DIAMOND
          Ok.

Diamond walks away with an expletive under her breath. Ani shrugs it off.

                    ANI
          Ok.

OMITTED

OMITTED

INT. HEADQUARTERS - LOCKER ROOM - NIGHT - LATER

Ani is eating dinner from a tupperware container while scrolling on her phone(in a super distinctive blinged out pink phone case). Lulu is sitting in front of the mirror next to two other dancers. They are doing their make-up and vaping.

ANI
Dude, the DJ is a fuckin' asshole.
I swear to god.

LULU
He's Jimmy's cousin. That's the
only reason he has this gig.

ANI
Fucking attitude on this guy. I
gave him my playlist and he said
maybe. Fucking maybe.

LULU
And how old is he? Like 40? Shit.

JIMMY (50) HQ's owner and DAWN (30), HQ's manager, enter the
dressing room.

JIMMY
Ani.

Ani doesn't want to answer.

ANI
Yeah?

JIMMY
Got a kid that wants someone who
knows Russian.

ANI
Your cousin better show some
respect around here or he ain't
getting shit from the girls.

JIMMY
I'll talk with him. C'mon.

ANI
I'm so deadass right now, Jimmy.

JIMMY
Seriously, what? What do you want
me to do?

ANI
He gave me attitude when I gave him
my playlist.

JIMMY
That's it? Attitude? I'm so sorry
your feelings are hurt but I don't
really give a care. Alright?
(MORE)

                    JIMMY (CONT'D)
          I'm dealing with a lot of straight
          up BS tonight. Let's go.

                    ANI
          I'm eating here.

                    DAWN
          That's why you have tupperware, to
          keep things fresh. C'mon.

                    LULU
          Where's what's-her-name?

                    DAWN
          Who? Katya? She's been gone for
          three months.

                    JIMMY
          Lulu... mind your own business.

                    ANI
          Jimmy.

                    JIMMY
          He's a spender. Let's go.

INT. HEADQUARTERS - MAIN ROOM - CONTINUOUS

Ani and JIMMY arrive at table twelve where IVAN (21) is
sitting with his friend ALEKS (20's, Russian-American), who
is already in conversation with another dancer.

                    JIMMY
          Gentlemen, please meet Ani. She'll
          take care of you tonight. Let me
          know if you need anything.

                    ANI
          Hey, I'm Ani.

                    IVAN
          Ivan.
               (Russian)
          Sit down, sit down. You're a
          beautiful girl.

Ani sits next to Ivan.

                    ANI
          Thank you.

                    IVAN
               (Russian)
          You speak Russian, right?

                    ANI
          I don't speak Russian but I know
          Russian.

Ivan is confused.

                    ANI (CONT'D)
          I can speak Russian but I'd just
          prefer not to. But you go ahead,
          speak Russian. I can understand.

                    IVAN
          I don't understand.

                    ANI
               (Russian)
          Ok, hello Ivan. I'm Ani. This is
          how I speak Russian. (beat) Do you
          still want me to speak Russian?

They both laugh.

                    ANI (CONT'D)
          You see? I'm terrible.

                    IVAN
          You're not bad.

                    ANI
          Well thank you but I disagree.

                    IVAN
          So how do you know Russian then?

                    ANI
          My grandmother never learned
          English so... But enough about me.
          You two from Russia?

                    IVAN
          I am. He lives here.

                    ANI
          Cool. On vacation?

                    IVAN
          Yes. I guess you could say that.
          I'm speaking Russian, ok?

                    ANI
          Whatever you want.

                    IVAN
               (Russian)
          Ok. Because I probably sound
          terrible in English.

                    ANI
          You're not bad.

                    IVAN
               (Russian)
          You need a drink so we can cheers
          to our bad accents.

                    ANI
          I'd love one.

                    IVAN
               (Russian)
          Let's get a bottle.

                    ANI
          Want to bring it to VIP?

INT. HEADQUARTERS - PRIVATE ROOM - NIGHT

Ani gives Ivan a dirty lap dance.

During the dance, Ivan places a $100 bill in Ani's bikini bottom strap. Ani turns it up a notch. Ivan places another $100 bill in the strap, she turns around and straddles him, reaches back and removes her top.

                    ANI
          No touching, ok?

                    IVAN
               (smiling)
          No touching.

She rides for a little while and then... another $100 bill. She smiles and spins around. Now sitting on his lap, she grabs his hands and places them on her breasts as she continues to grind back into him.

When the fourth $100 bill is offered...

                    ANI
          Ok, can you sit on your hands for
          me?

                    IVAN
          Sit on my hands?

                    ANI
          Yeah, hands under your legs.

Ivan complies.

                    ANI (CONT'D)
          And you gotta keep them there ok?
               (Russian)
          This is a no-no. But I like you.

Ivan nods. Ani stands, turns and removes her bottoms.
Twirling the thong around on her finger, she sits and
straddles. Ivan is losing his mind.

INT. HEADQUARTERS - UPSTAIRS COUCHES - NIGHT

Ivan and Ani are lounging on one of the black leather
couches. One her legs is up over his. They toast and do a
shot of vodka. Ivan says his cheers in Russian and talks Ani
into toasting in Russian as well.

                    IVAN
               (Russian)
          Do you work outside the club?

Ani knows what he's asking.

                    ANI
          Give me your phone.

Ivan gives Ani his phone, unlocking it as he passes it to
her. Ani puts her contact in the phone. And hands it back to
him.

                    ANI (CONT'D)
          Text me.

INT. SUBWAY CAR - DAWN

The sun has not risen yet but the sky is beginning to lighten
as Ani rides the subway by herself, barely staying awake. She
arrives at the Brighton Beach train station.

EXT. SUBWAY STATION - DAWN

Ani exits the station as five commuters in business attire
are entering.

EXT. BRIGHTON BEACH AVENUE - EARLY MORNING

Ani walks the almost empty streets from the subway station to her apartment building.

EXT. BRIGHTON BEACH AVENUE - EARLY MORNING

She approaches her apartment building and walks up the front steps.

INT. ANI'S APARTMENT - BEDROOM - DAY

Bright daylight pours through the window. Ani is sound asleep wearing an eye mask. A knock on her door. VERA (25), Ani's sister enters.

VERA
Yo. Yo.

Ani starts to stir.

VERA (CONT'D)
Did you pick up milk?

Ani wakes and pulls the mask down. Annoyed, she looks at her sister.

ANI
Do you see milk in the fridge?

VERA
No.

ANI
Then I didn't pick up the fucking milk.

Vera slams the door. Ani puts the mask back on and turns over.

EXT. MANSION (MILL BASIN) - DAY

Ivan's huge waterfront MANSION sits behind a privacy gate manned by a security booth. Ani's Uber arrives at the address and she steps out. She approaches the DAY GUARD.

ANI
Hello. I'm here for Mr. Zakharov.

DAY GUARD
Ivan?

                              ANI
                    Yeah.

                              DAY GUARD
                    Your name?

                              ANI
                    Ani

The guard confirms her name on his iPad and opens the gate.

EXT. MANSION DRIVEWAY/ENTRANCE - DAY

Ani walks through the gate and approaches the mansion. She is impressed. She rings the doorbell. Ivan answers with boyish excitement.

                              IVAN
                        (Russian)
                    Hello. Welcome. Come in.

INT. MANSION - FOYER - CONTINUOUS

Ani enters, taking in the gorgeous home. The first floor features an oversized kitchen, living area and dining room, double height foyer and a separate large office space. Floor to ceiling windows provide water views.

Ivan takes Ani's coat and hangs it in a closet near the front door.

                              IVAN
                        (Russian)
                    Want something to drink?

                              ANI
                    I'll take a water.

                              IVAN
                        (Russian)
                    Water? You sure? You can have
                    anything you want. Vodka? Tequila?
                    Coca-Cola?

                              ANI
                    Water's good.

Ivan walks towards the kitchen leaving Ani in the foyer.

                    IVAN
              (Russian)
        Ok, suit yourself. Sparkling or
        flat?

                    ANI
        Either is good.

Ani is overwhelmed with the space.

                    ANI (CONT'D)
        Wow. Not too shabby.

Ivan approaches with a bottle of VOSS water.

                    IVAN
        What is "not too shabby?"

                    ANI
        Oh... beautiful. Your home is
        beautiful.

                    IVAN
              (Russian)
        Yeah? Ok.
              (hands her the water)
        Sparkling.

                    ANI
        Thank you.

                    IVAN
              (boyishly points up)
        Bedroom's upstairs.

                                              CUT TO:

INT. MANSION - FOYER/STAIRWAY - DAY

Ivan leads Ani upstairs to the master bedroom.

INT. MANSION - MASTER BEDROOM - CONTINUOUS

They enter the beautiful room. The bed donned with designer sheets is unmade. Ani walks towards the window overlooking the basin.

                    IVAN
        Excuse the mess. They haven't fixed
        my bed yet... (to self, as he tries
        to tidy the bed) Is it so
        difficult?

                    ANI
          Nice view.

                    IVAN
          My view is better.

Ani turns to see Ivan ogling her body. She chuckles.

                    ANI
          Ok.
               (beat)
          So what are you looking for?

                    IVAN
          Sex.

                    ANI
               (chuckling)
          Yeah, I know. I mean... anything
          special?

                    IVAN
          Yeah, special sex.

                    ANI
          Special sex. So... a little bit of
          everything.

                    IVAN
               (Russian)
          That sounds special. Yeah.

                                        SMASH CUT TO:

Ani finishes removing her clothes. Ivan watches.

                    ANI
          Want to take your clothes off?

                    IVAN
          Yes, I do.

Ivan strips in seconds.

                    ANI
               (looking at his crotch)
          Ready to go. Alright.

Ani seductively pushes Ivan down so he's seated on the side of the bed. She takes a condom from the bedside table.

                    ANI (CONT'D)
          Do you want to put this on or do
          you want me to put in on for you?

Ivan motions for her to do it. Ani tears open the condom wrapper with her teeth and removes it. Ani puts the condom on Ivan.

                ANI (CONT'D)
    There we go.

She starts by kissing his chest, moving to his nipples, down to his stomach...

                IVAN
        (Russian)
    Wait, I need to do it right now.

INT. MANSION - MASTER BEDROOM - SECONDS LATER

Ani and Ivan are having sex. Ivan is like a jackrabbit. Ani is slightly amused by his boyish enthusiasm and lack of finesse.

                          CUT TO:

INT. MANSION - MASTER BEDROOM - LATER

Ivan is dabbing. He points to cash on the bedside table.

                IVAN
    That's for you. Tip.

Ani takes it and flips through the bills. There's a lot.

                ANI
    Oh, wow. Thank you.

As Ivan is exhaling...

                IVAN
        (Russian)
    That was amazing.

                ANI
    Very nice of you.

Ivan smiles and dabs again.

                IVAN
    You want?

Ani takes the dab and smokes. Ivan hits a button on the wall and a television slowly rises from the console in front of the bed while Ani and Ivan talk. A music video channel plays on the television.

ANI
How old are you?

IVAN
21. You?

ANI
Older than you.

IVAN
(Russian)
What are you like... 25?

ANI
23!

IVAN
(Russian)
You act like a 25-year-old.

ANI
You're funny.

IVAN
Funny? Why?

ANI
I don't know, you're just funny.

IVAN
Funny cool, right?

ANI
Yeah, funny cool.
   (beat)
So what do you do to... get all this?

IVAN
(Russian)
What do you think I do?

ANI
What do you think I think you do?

IVAN
I'm big drug dealer.

ANI
Really?

                    IVAN
          No.
               (beat)
          I'm big guns dealer.

                    ANI
          Really?

                    IVAN
          No.

                    ANI
          You made some app or something?

                    IVAN
               (Russian)
          I do have some cool ideas for apps
          but no.

Ani waits for the real answer.

                    ANI
          So?

Ivan answers in a way that indicates he is not exactly proud.

                    IVAN
               (Russian)
          My father is Nikolai Zakharov.

Ani doesn't know who that is.

                    IVAN (CONT'D)
          Google him.

Ani takes out her phone.

                    ANI
          What's his name again?

                    IVAN
          Nikolai Zakharov. Z. A. K. H...

Ani types away. She stares at the screen.

                    ANI
          Got it. Oh.
               (beat)
          Oh.

We see the Wiki Page of NIKOLAI ZAKHAROV. Ivan leans over and points at the screen.

                    IVAN
               (Russian)
          Yeah, see there. Children. Ivan
          Zakharov. That's me.

                    ANI
          Oh shit.

INT. HEADQUARTERS - LOCKER ROOM - NIGHT

Lulu is looking at Ani's phone with her jaw dropped. Ani is
visibly happy.

                    LULU
          Oh shit.

                    ANI
          Yeah. And... seeing him again
          tomorrow.

                    LULU
          No way.

                    ANI
          Yeah... guess he had fun.

Ani notices Diamond listening in. Diamond is sipping
Strawberry Yoo-hoo from a glass bottle with a straw.

                    ANI (CONT'D)
          Want to mind your business?

                    DIAMOND
          You're makin' it our business.
               (Diamond turns away and
                under her breath...)
          Chatty bitch.

Diamond looks Ani straight in the eyes as she slowly and
obnoxiously slurps the last of the Yoo-hoo. Ani stares back.
Dawn enters.

                    DAWN
          Ok, which one of you decided to
          bedazzle my clipboard?

                    LULU
          Oh that's cute.

                    DAWN
          Whoever did this owes me a new
          clipboard.

INT. MANSION - LIVING ROOM - DAY

Wearing a thong, netted top and pleasers, Ani crawls across the living room floor. She's giving an erotic dance, similar to the way she would if on a club's stage. She turns and crawls back toward the couch. We reveal that we are in Ivan's living room. Ani crawls up and on to Ivan where she removes her top.

INT. MANSION - LIVING ROOM - DAY - LATER

        IVAN
    (Russian)
That was crazy good. You're the best.

Ani smirks, amused and flattered.

Ivan is playing video games and dabbing. He passes it to her.

        IVAN (CONT'D)
    (Russian)
Hey, you should come to my New Year's party.
    (English)
It's going to be bangin'.

Ani smiles.

        ANI
I might have to work that night.

        IVAN
    (Russian)
You might not have to work that night.
    (beat)

        ANI
Can I bring someone?

        IVAN
    (Russian)
Not if it's a guy.
    (English)
I don't want a sausage party.

        ANI
She's not.

        IVAN
    (Russian)
Ok, then. See you here.

                    ANI
          So you paid for an hour and there's
          still like 45 minutes if you want
          to go again.

                    IVAN
               (Russian)
          Oh shit, yeah!

                                        CUT TO:

Another jackrabbit session. Ani can't help but laugh when he climaxes in seconds.

INT. UBER BACKSEAT - NIGHT

Ani and Lulu are having fun being mischievous and doing bumps of coke in the backseat of the Uber.

EXT. MILL BASIN - STREET - NIGHT

Ani and Lulu exit an Uber. They are dressed to the nines in high heels and clothes way too skimpy for the freezing weather. They hear the pulsing bass from the party. A MANSION BOUNCER and the NIGHT GUARD checks them in.

They approach the house which radiates colored light.

                    LULU
               (in awe)
          No way.

There are partyers visible in all the windows. Two very intoxicated partyers sit on the steps outside.

EXT. MANSION - DOORWAY - NIGHT

The two approach the front door... music pounding.

                    LULU
          Oh shit. (whispers) Can you adjust
          my tits? I think my tits are off.

Ani jumps to the rescue. The door opens in mid fix. Two guys exit with drinks in hand. Ani and Lulu enter the house.

INT. MANSION - NIGHT - CONTINUOUS

The place is packed with partiers... drinking, smoking and dancing.

Ivan who is trying his hand at DJ'ing spots Ani. He makes a
beeline for them. The DJ steps back in.

                    IVAN
               (English)
     Hey... New York's hottest girl is
     here!

The girls laugh.

                    ANI
     This is my friend Lulu.

Ivan is very charming. He gets on one knee and kisses her
hand. The girls laugh.

                                      CUT TO:

INT. MANSION - NIGHT - LATER

Ivan is the king of the party. TOM (early 20's, Russian-
American) and Aleks are the two friends we see the most with
Ivan. Alek's girlfriend DASHA (24) is also present.

Ivan is helping the girls to take shots from the ice
sculpture (a voluptuous woman's bust). Aleks is nearby and
notices Ani from the club.

                    ALEKS
     Hey! I know you! Happy New Year!

Ani introduces Lulu to Aleks. Aleks intro's Dasha.

INT. MANSION - NIGHT - LATER

Aleks and Dasha are out of earshot of Ani and Lulu.

                    DASHA
     (Russian)
     How do you know them?

                    ALEKS
     (Russian)
     That's the escort Ivan is fucking.

INT. MANSION - NIGHT- LATER

Ivan leads a drinking game. Ani and Lulu watch him. The girls
are having a great time.

INT. MANSION - NIGHT - LATER

Ani is dancing with Lulu, putting the other dancers to shame.

                LULU
        (screaming over the music)
  Does he have a brother?

                ANI
        (screaming over the music)
  Happy New Year's, bitch.

INT. MANSION - THIRD FLOOR - LATER

Ani and Lulu explore upstairs.

INT. MANSION - FAMILY ROOM - LATER

MUSIC IS BLASTING and DISCO LIGHTS ARE PULSATING. In the FAMILY ROOM/LIVING ROOM AREA, Ani, Lulu, Ivan and his party entourage/hanger-ons are draped over a large, extravagant couch. Lots of open drug-use. Champagne flows and shots of vodka are being poured. Everyone is having fun. During the chaos, Ani and Ivan toast their champagne glasses.

On the other side of the room, Tom's sister CRYSTAL (18, little sister-type) jumps on Ivan and tries to make out with him. Ivan pushes her away.

                IVAN
        (screaming over music)
  Whoa, whoa, whoa. I'm a taken man
  already.

                CRYSTAL
  Oh really?

                IVAN
  This is Ani. Ani, this...

                CRYSTAL
  Crystal.

                IVAN
  Crystal.

                ANI
  Hi.

                CRYSTAL
  Hey. Well cool.

Crystal awkwardly exits the moment.

Ivan leans into Ani so he doesn't have to yell.

                    IVAN
               (Russian)
          Thank you.
               (referring to Crystal)
          She's a little...
               (he indicates "crazy")

                    ANI
          Anytime.

                    IVAN
               (Russian)
          You look great.

                    ANI
          Thank you.
               (beat)
          You were right. This is bangin'.

                    IVAN
               (Russian)
          Having fun?

                    ANI
          Yeah.

                    IVAN
               (Russian)
          Are you available tonight?

                    ANI
          Maybe.

                    IVAN
          Maybe?

                    ANI
          Well it's New Year's Eve.

                    IVAN
               (Russian)
          Yeah?

Ani thinks about it for a moment.

                    ANI
               (whispering)
          I have holiday rates.

Ivan smiles.

                    IVAN
              (Russian)
          I'm glad you came.

                    ANI
          Me too.

INT. MANSION - LIVING ROOM - LATER

The Times Square ball drop coverage is on the large TV in the living room. Aleks jumps up on a nearby couch.

                    ALEKS
          Oh shit! It's almost midnight!
              (Russian) It's almost midnight.

This gets everyone's attention. Behind them, in the KITCHEN AREA, two men stand out in the midst of the youthful party. TOROS (50's, Armenian-American) and GARNIK (40's, Armenian-American) monitor the proceedings with their arms crossed.

                    TOROS
          Hey, this is not a jungle gym, get
          off of there.

Aleks complies.

                    TOROS (CONT'D)
          Fucking kids.

The countdown begins. The kids are screaming 10, 9, 8...

INT. MANSION - BALCONY - LATER

The crowd is watching fireworks in the distance. They light up the NYC skyline with every color. Tom offers everyone swigs from the champagne bottle. Using the fire pit to light, Ivan and his buddies shoot roman candles off the balcony. Ani and Lulu join in.

                                             CUT TO:

INT. MANSION - MASTER BEDROOM - LATER

Ani is riding on top of Ivan.

                    ANI
          That feel good?

Ivan can barely respond, he's in such bliss. Suddenly, a knock on the door. Ani stops humping.

                    IVAN
              Yeah?

                    TOROS (O.S.)
                    (Russian)
              Ivan, we're leaving. You good?

                    IVAN
                    (Russian)
              Whatever. I'm busy, man. The fuck.

Ivan gives a "pay no mind" look to Ani.

                    ANI
                    (after a beat)
              All good?

                    IVAN
              All's great.

Ani starts up again.

                                              CUT TO:

INT. MANSION - MASTER BEDROOM - LATE AFTERNOON

It's New Year's Day. The bright orange low winter sun shines on Ani's face causing her to wake. Slowly coming to, she looks at her phone.

                    ANI
                    (amused)
              Oh shit.

Ani looks over at the sleeping Ivan. She gets out of bed and starts dressing. Ivan wakes up.

                    IVAN
              Good morning.

                    ANI
              No, no dude, it's 5 o'clock... PM.

                    IVAN
                    (Russian)
              Oh good afternoon. Well, come back.
              C'mon. Don't go yet.

                    ANI
              Dude, I work tonight. I got shit to
              do.

IVAN
(Russian)
Here, come back. Please. Just a minute.

He pats the bed. Ani plays along and sits. Ivan looks at her but doesn't say anything.

ANI
Yeah?

IVAN
(Russian)
So... I want you to be exclusive with me. For the week. And we can have... fun.

Ani is fluent in Russian yet still struggles especially with larger words.

ANI
What's
(Russian)
'exclusive'?

IVAN
I don't know... only with me.

ANI
Exclusive.

IVAN
Yes, exclusive.

ANI
Like how... exclusive?

IVAN
(Russian)
Hang with me and my boys for the week. We can have fun. Party. Like... be my girlfriend for the week.

Ani studies him.

IVAN (CONT'D)
(English)
My horny girlfriend for the week.

Ivan laughs at his own joke. Ani smirks.

                    IVAN (CONT'D)
              (Russian)
          No, but seriously.

Ani doesn't answer but makes the "pay me" gesture with her fingers.

                    IVAN (CONT'D)
              (Russian)
          Oh... of course... how about 10K
          for the week?

Ani takes a beat.

                    ANI
          15, cash, up front.

                    IVAN
          No problem.

Ani wasn't expecting that.

                    IVAN (CONT'D)
          So... deal?

                    ANI
          Deal.

Ani pauses and smirks

                    ANI (CONT'D)
          You know, I would have done it for
          10.

                    IVAN
              (Russian)
          I would have gone to 30.

Ani hits him playfully.

INT. MANSION - MASTER BEDROOM - AFTERNOON

Ani steps out of Ivan's room and walks through the mansion. We follow her downstairs. A man and two women from a cleaning service are working on the previous night's mess. Ani politely smiles at KLARA (27) when they make eye contact. She exits the front door.

INT. UBER - DUSK

In the back seat, Ani tries to hold in her excitement but it peeks through every so often.

INT. HEADQUARTERS - POLE ROOM - NIGHT

Ani pole dances for a group of guys out for a birthday celebration. She removes her top to transition into lap dancing. She moves from one guy to the next as they place bills in her bikini bottom.

INT. HEADQUARTERS - UPSTAIRS BAR - NIGHT

The guys are exiting the pole room. Ani hugs each guy as they exit. Dawn stands next to Ani.

DAWN
Come with me.

INT. HEADQUARTERS - HALLWAY - NIGHT

Ani, with Dawn in tow, walks down the hall, through the kitchen and towards office.

DAWN
He's not going to be happy. I'm telling you right now. He's not going to happy.

ANI
Oh please.

INT. HEADQUARTERS - HQ KITCHEN - NIGHT

Ani and Dawn enter.

ANI
Hey Jimmy.

Jimmy spins in his office chair.

DAWN
Go ahead. Tell him.

Ani is about to speak.

DAWN (CONT'D)
Tell him. Cause I don't want to.

ANI
I am Dawn. Thank you.

JIMMY
Whoa. Whoa. What's going on?

                    DAWN
          What's going on is she wants a week
          off. That's what's going on.

                    ANI
          I thought you wanted me to tell
          him.

                    DAWN
          You see what I deal with. I had the
          schedule done... already
          distributed. And she pulls this
          last minute.

                    JIMMY
          What? We just gave you New Year's.

                    ANI
          Jesus Christ Jimmy. When I'm
          getting health insurance, worker's
          comp and a fucking 401k, you can
          tell me when I work and not work.

                    JIMMY
          Thank you Ani! Love you! Thank you
          very much.

INT. HEADQUARTERS - HALLWAY - NIGHT

Ani walks away from the door.

                    ANI
          Um, I don't know what you're
          talking about, but anyway I'm not
          taking any more shifts this week.

                    JIMMY
          Thank you Ani! Love you! Thank you
          very much.

INT. ANI'S APARTMENT - DAY

Ani swings a duffle bag over her shoulder and passes by her Vera who is sitting on the couch watching TV but glued to her phone. Vera's boyfriend VLAD (late 20's) is splayed out on the couch next to her.

                    ANI
          Back next Tuesday.

                    VERA
          Today is Tuesday.

                    ANI
          Correct. And I'll be back next
          Tuesday.

                    VERA
          That's a week.

                    ANI
          You got that right.

The door shuts hard behind her.

EXT. ANI'S APARTMENT - DAY

Ani walks down steps with luggage and into a black car Uber.

ANI/IVAN/FRIENDS PARTYING MONTAGE.

The next section shows us the crazy fun week that Ani has with Ivan. Ani is physically close to Ivan at all times, giving him the "girlfriend experience".

Ani plays video games with Ivan and his friends.

They have a pile of pizza boxes and bags of candy, etc.

They party at VIP tables at NYC's best clubs.

(We show 7 club interiors and 4 exteriors)

INT. MANSION - MASTER BEDROOM - NIGHT

Ani and Ivan have sex in the master bedroom.

INT. MANSION - SAUNA - DAY

Ani and Ivan have sex in the sauna.

INT. MANSION - FATHER'S OFFICE - DAY

Ani and Ivan have sex on the rug of the upstairs office.

INT. MANSION - DAY

Ani and Ivan have sex in the shower.

INT. MANSION - MASTER BEDROOM - DAY

Ani and Ivan have sex in the master bedroom.

OMITTED

EXT. BOARDWALK - DAY

Ani and Ivan walk up on to the boardwalk toward the smoke shop.

INT. VAPE SHOP - DAY

Ani and Ivan hang at the Vape Shop managed by Tom. Crystal and Aleks are there as well. They smoke... a lot.

EXT. CONEY ISLAND BEACH - DAY

Ani, Ivan, Crystal, Tom and Aleks are high, laughing and watching a polar bear swimmer in the cold water. Crystal and Ani are watching the guys rough house.

CRYSTAL
So you're Russian?

ANI
Well Russian-American I guess.

CRYSTAL
Born there?

ANI
Yeah but I been here since I was three.

CRYSTAL
That's cool. Yeah, I'm Russian... but I was born here. (Beat) Sucks.

Ani is amused.

ANI
How old are you?

CRYSTAL
17.

ANI
And you two are dating?

Ani points to Tom. Crystal bursts out laughing.

                    CRYSTAL
          Tom? (laughing) No! He's my cousin.
          (to the guys in Russian) Hey... Ani
          thought Tom and I are dating.

The guys think this is the funniest thing they ever heard.
Ani is very confused. Finally...

                    IVAN
          They're cousins!

INT. MANSION - RANDOM BEDROOM - DAY

Ani and Ivan get a couples massage.

OMITTED

INT. MANSION - MASTER BEDROOM - NIGHT

Ani and Ivan lounge naked on the bed smoking and watching a movie.

INT. MANSION - LIVING ROOM - DAY

A cleaning staff works around Ani and Ivan lounging on the couch. The two lift their legs for the vacuum.

                    IVAN
               (Russian)
          Klara, you want a hit?

Ivan offers the dab to her and she smiles.

                    KLARA
               (Russian)
          Not today, Mr. Zakharov.

Ivan turns to Ani.

                    IVAN
               (English)
          The last time Klara smoked, my mom
          caught her doing a cryo session.

                    KLARA
          What did you say?

                    IVAN
              (Russian)
         Nothing. I promise.

They all laugh.

                    ANI
         Wait, you have a cryo chamber?

                    IVAN
              (Russian) Yeah, my mom thinks it
         makes her younger. Want to try?

INT. MANSION - GARAGE - DAY

The two walk through the garage. Ani has a towel draped around her. They both wear flip-flops. They walk by a PORSCHE, ROLLS ROYCE and MERCEDES JEEP.

                    IVAN
         I got the keys confiscated because
         I brought the Porsche to a take-
         over and fucked up the bumper.
              (beat) My parents are assholes.

INT. MANSION - BASEMENT - DAY

Ani stands in a cryo chamber engulfed in flowing steam. She is shivering as they both laugh.

OMITTED

OMITTED

INT. MANSION - ZODIAC ROOM - NIGHT

Mid-week, Tom, Aleks, Dasha and Crystal are hanging in the house. Lines of powder spin from person to person on the Lazy Susan.

                    CRYSTAL
         Is this coke or K?

                    ANI
         Calvin Klein.

                    DASHA
          (Russian)
     The best K I've ever had was in
     Vegas.

                    IVAN
     Great idea. Let's go to Vegas right
     now!

INT. PRIVATE JET - DAY

Ani, Ivan, Tom, Aleks, Dasha and Crystal, take a private
flight to Las Vegas. Ivan and Ani are sipping champagne. Ivan
chats away in Russian about a cool DJ set he saw the other
night.

Ani sips her drink while watching the face of the flight
attendant eating from tupperware in the kitchen area.

INT. CAESARS PALACE - LOBBY - EVENING

The opulent lobby of Caesar's Palace-- the chandeliers,
bright lights, statues and columns are pure Vegas. A HOTEL
MANAGER approaches Ivan.

                    HOTEL MANAGER
     Welcome back to Caesars Palace, Mr.
     Zakharov. Your suite is just about
     ready. We didn't know you were
     coming and the suite was occupied
     but they're out and housekeeping
     should be done any minute.

                    IVAN
     What the fuck, man. You mean I have
     to wait...

The hotel manager doesn't know how to reply.

                    IVAN (CONT'D)
          (with a big smile)
     I'm fucking with you, man! No
     problem. We'll be on the floor!
     It's great to be back!

                                                  CUT TO:

INT. CAESAR'S PALACE - PENTHOUSE - NIGHT

They enter their stunning suite. Everyone is very impressed.

                    CRYSTAL
               (to Ani)
          What a life, right?

                                             CUT TO:

INT. CAESAR'S PALACE - PENTHOUSE - MASTER BEDROOM - NIGHT

Ani enters the bedroom with some sexy lingerie and
seductively crawls on to the bed.

                                       SMASH CUT TO:

Ani and Ivan have fun sex.

                                             CUT TO:

INT. CASINO - HIGH ROLLERS TABLE - LATER

Ivan loses 200K gambling. They laugh about it.

                                             CUT TO:

INT. LAS VEGAS - CLUB - NIGHT

Dancing and drinking bottled water and taking bumps of coke
and K.

                                             CUT TO:

INT. CAESAR'S PALACE - PENTHOUSE - DAY

Ivan and Ani are getting hangover IV's. A nurse sits nearby.
Ani is loving every minute of it.

                                             CUT TO:

EXT. LAS VEGAS - ROOFTOP POOL - DAY

Ivan and Ani have a splash fight while holding their fancy
cocktails.

                                             CUT TO:

INT. NOBU RESTAURANT - DINING ROOM - EVENING

A hip and fun crowd gather at the Las Vegas hot spot.

The crew enjoy a huge and elaborate sushi platter and drink bottles of sake.

                              CUT TO:

INT. CAESAR'S PALACE - PENTHOUSE - NIGHT

The crew returns from a crazy night. They run through the penthouse like kids.

EXT. CAESAR'S PALACE - PENTHOUSE BALCONY - NIGHT

Looking over the city, Ani smokes a cigarette and Crystal vapes. Off in the background, Dasha and Aleks are having an argument in Russian.

                    DASHA
              (Russian)
          Yeah right you would.

She storms off and Aleks follows. Crystal, in show off mode, turns to Ani.

                    CRYSTAL
          I bet they're going to have make-up
          sex.

                    ANI
          And it's going to be crazy.

They laugh.

                    CRYSTAL
          You know... I only fuck FOB's.

                    ANI
          Oh yeah? (amused) How many FOB's
          have you fucked?

                    CRYSTAL
          I mean... well my ex was a FOB and
          he's the only guy I've ever
          fucked... but you know, I plan to
          only fuck FOB's moving forward.

                    ANI
          Cool. (beat) They can be fun.

INT. CAESAR'S PALACE - PENTHOUSE - BEDROOM - NIGHT

Ivan is behind Ani, once again pounding away like a jackrabbit.

                    ANI
      Ok, hold on. You know... it could
      last longer and be better if you
      take it easy. Here... just let me.

She takes control and shows him how it's done.

                                   CUT TO:

INT. CAESAR'S PALACE - PENTHOUSE - BEDROOM - MINUTES LATER

Ani and Ivan are in bed post-coital.

                    ANI
      I hope you had fun this week.

                    IVAN
      I hope you had fun this week.

                    ANI
      I did.
        (beat)
      We should do it again sometime.

They lie there for a moment.

                    IVAN
        (Russian)
      I leave to go back to Russia at the
      end of the month. I promised my dad
      that I'd start working for his
      company.

                    ANI
      Oh... it all makes sense now.

They laugh.

                ANI (CONT'D)
      I'm gonna miss you. Does that sound
      weird?

                    IVAN
      You'll miss me or my money?

                    ANI
      Money, of course.

They laugh.

                    IVAN
          If I got married to an American, I
          would never have to go back.

                    ANI
          Yeah, who would you marry?

                    IVAN
          I don't know... Crystal? Your
          friend Lulu? She's hot.

They laugh.

                    IVAN (CONT'D)
          You?

                    ANI
               (mocking his accent)
          You?

They laugh.

                    IVAN
          It is Vegas. Don't people get
          married in Vegas?

                    ANI
          Don't fuck around.

                    IVAN
          I'm not fucking around.

                    ANI
          Ok, well then go get married.

                    IVAN
          Ok. Let's get married.

                    ANI
          You asshole.

                    IVAN
          What?

                    ANI
          Don't tease me with that shit. That
          ain't cool.

Ivan waits a moment.

                    IVAN
          Will you marry me?

                    ANI
          Seriously?

                    IVAN
          Seriously.

                    ANI
          You want to marry... you want to
          get married?

                    IVAN
               (Russian)
          Because I like what we have going
          on here and I think you do too... I
          think you'd like it even if you
          weren't paid to. (English) And I
          become American! And my parents can
          go screw!

Ani processes.

                    ANI
          You're serious.

                    IVAN
          Yes, I'm serious. I said I'm
          serious.

Ani considers it for what seems like forever. Finally she waves her left hand drawing attention to her ring finger.

                    ANI
          Three carats.

                    IVAN
          I'd look terrible if you had
          anything under four.

Ani's smile is a mile wide.

                                        CUT TO:

MONTAGE. LAS VEGAS MARRIAGE. VARIOUS LOCATIONS.

I/E. WEDDING CHAPEL - NIGHT

Next thing they know, Ani and Ivan are running through the Las Vegas streets to a WEDDING CHAPEL. They get married.

EXT. FREMONT ST. - NIGHT

They party the next day, celebrating the marriage, ending the day at the FREMONT STREET EXPERIENCE saluting under a dancing light show and "God Bless the USA" plays.

CUT TO:

INT. PRIVATE JET - DAY

They are on the jet headed back to NYC. Ivan, Tom, Aleks, Dasha and Crystal are passed out. Ani studies Ivan. The harsh sunlight creeps up Ivan's face. Ani sees this. She reaches over and pulls down the window shade.

CUT TO:

INT. HEADQUARTERS - LOCKER ROOM - NIGHT

Ani is clearing out her locker. Lulu, Jimmy and Dawn are present. There are three other dancers in the room including SUNNY (21). Everyone is happy for Ani. Dawn, who hangs in the back, is the only one looking a little sour.

                    SUNNY
    Oh my god. You're so lucky.

                    LULU
    You hit the jackpot, bitch.

                    JIMMY
    She hit the Lotto, PowerBall and
    Mega Millions, bitch.

They laugh.

                    ANI
    I'll come back and visit you guys.
    Get myself a private or two.

They laugh.

                    JIMMY
    So this is for real? Because if so,
    I got to stop letting high rollers
    in. They're stealing my girls.

They laugh. Ani zips up her bag. The gang hugs and says goodbye. Ani passes Dawn. They look at each other.

                    DAWN
    Come here kid.

They hug.

                    ANI
          Love you Dawn.

                    DAWN
          I'll miss ya kid.

                                        CUT TO:

INT. HEADQUARTERS - VARIOUS - MOMENTS LATER

Ani walks toward the door with her packed bag. Lulu walks
aside her, proud of her friend. Ani runs over and hugs a few
friends near the bar. Near the entrance, she passes Diamond
who is standing near the door.

                    DIAMOND
          Got your whale?

Ani stops and slowly turns.

                    ANI
          Seems I did. Didn't I?

                    DIAMOND
          I give it two weeks, bitch.

The two women are in each other's faces.

                    LULU
          Hey hey hey.

It's all about to explode... when Ani suddenly grabs
Diamond's head and plants a big fat obnoxious kiss on the
lips. Diamond immediately reacts and pushes Ani away. Ani
laughs. Diamond lunges forward but Lulu and the HQ SECURITY
GUARD jumps in before she can connect. Ani exits into the
night.

INT. ANI'S APARTMENT - HALLWAY - DAY

Ani is dragging two large pieces of luggage out of the
doorway.

                    VERA
          He married you for a green card.

                    ANI
          Whatever. It's not about a green
          card. He could easily buy
          citizenship.

                    VERA
          But you're getting him a green
          card.

                    ANI
          It's not about the green card. He
          likes living here in America...
          with me.

                    VERA
          How well do you know him?

                    ANI
          How well do I know him... did you
          hear what I said? Try to keep up.
          His dad is loaded... Nikolai
          Zakharov. Fucking Google him. He's
          worth 22... billion.
          BILLLLLIIOOOONNNN.

She waits for her sister's reaction. She's still processing.

                    ANI (CONT'D)
          Don't worry. I'll keep paying the
          rent. Understand? Ok? Ok. Bye.

The door closes and Vera looks at Vlad who is planted on the
couch.

                    VLAD
               (Russian)
          Did she say billion?

                                                  CUT TO:

MONTAGE. ANI "BECOMING MRS." VARIOUS LOCATIONS.

I/E. RING SHOP - DAY

We see Ivan and Ani shopping for wedding rings.

I/E FUR SHOP - DAY

They pass by a fur shop. They eye the black Russian sable
winter coat in the window.

                                                  CUT TO:

40.

EXT. SIDEWALK - DAY

Ani is wearing the coat as they walk down the sidewalk.

CUT TO:

INT. MANSION - DAY

Ani moves into the mansion. She places a few picture frames in the bedroom. One of her with her sister and mother. Another with Lulu and friends. She fills the bathroom with her products and the closet with her clothes. She quickly becomes very comfortable in her new home.

Ani admires Ivan's mother's closet. It's huge and is lined with designer clothes, shoes and handbags. She sees a designer eye mask.

CUT TO:

They are having sex in the closet.

INT. MANSION - BATHROOM - DUSK

Ani smokes a blunt in her bubble bath.

EXT. MANSION - BALCONY - DUSK

Ani and Ivan are out on the balcony smoking cigars. They both wear expensive, plush white bathrobes. They hold and kiss each other in romantic, domestic bliss.

We pull out from the house (helicopter shot) to show the expanse of the property and Manhattan in the distance.

CUT TO:

EXT. ARMENIAN CHURCH - NEW YORK CITY - DAY

A crowd is entering the church for a baptism.

INT. ARMENIAN CHURCH - BACKROOM - DAY

Toros is on his cellphone.

                TOROS
           (Russian)
     This can't be true. Impossible.

The priest stands in the background slightly concerned. We hear the voices of Ivan's father NIKOLAI ZAKHAROV (56) and Ivan's mother, GALINA ZAKHAROV (41) screaming on the other end.

>   TOROS (CONT'D)
>   (Russian)
>   No, let me assure you, this is
>   impossible. These are just rumors.
>   I was with him on New Year's Eve,
>   he isn't married.

Toros is starting to sweat.

>   TOROS (CONT'D)
>   (Russian)
>   No, no, no disrespect. Of course.
>   Ok. But it can't be true.
>   (beat)
>   No, I'm at... I'm not there right
>   now but I'm headed there.
>   (he looks to the priest
>   and shakes his head.)
>   I will let you know ASAP. You'll
>   hear from me in 30 minutes max.
>   Yes, understood. Ok. Bye.

The gravity of this moment is sinking in.

>   TOROS (CONT'D)
>   FUCK!

He's so pissed he can only half apologize to the priest.

INT. ARMENIAN CHURCH - MOMENTS LATER

Toros walks out into the main area of the church where the family and friends are finding their seats. He spots his right hand man GARNIK who's with his mother in the middle of one of the pews. He runs over and motions to him. TOROS'S WIFE (44, RUSSIAN) clocks this from across the room.

>   TOROS
>   (in a shouting whisper)
>   Garnik, I need you now. Come.

>   GARNIK
>   Now?

>   TOROS
>   Right now. It's an emergency.

42.

                    GARNIK
          Ivan?

                    TOROS
          Get over here.

Garnik gets up and squeezes by the other guests, annoying
everybody.

                    TOROS (CONT'D)
          Here.

He removes a key card from his set of keys and hands it to
Garnik.

                    TOROS (CONT'D)
                (Armenian)
          I need you to grab the Russian and
          get over to the house NOW!

Across the room...

Toros's wife turns to their son.

                    TOROS'S WIFE
          What is he up to?

INT. MANSION - LIVING ROOM - DAY

Ivan and Ani are nestled together on the couch. Ivan is
playing an online video game. The framing passes tightly over
them and reveals the 4-carat ring on Ani's finger. The shot
rests on Ani's face as she watches the video game.

We see the flash of a cell phone (off-screen) coming from the
coffee table. Ani looks at it.

                    ANI
                (Russian)
          Come on. Just answer or shut it
          off.

Ivan grabs the phone and turns it off.

                    IVAN
                (Russian)
          There. Off.

He settles back on to the couch and resumes the game.

                    ANI
          Ivan.

44.

>   IVAN
>   Yeah?
>
>   ANI
>   What did they say when you told
>   them?
>
>   IVAN
>   (Russian)
>   I don't want to talk about them.
>
>   ANI
>   You did tell them, right?
>
>   IVAN
>   Yeah sure.
>
>   ANI
>   I mean...
>   (Russian)
>   This is good news. Right? Parents
>   usually want their kids to get
>   married.
>
>   IVAN
>   (Russian)
>   Yeah, but my parents are dicks. And
>   whatever.
>
>   ANI
>   (Russian)
>   Well, no matter what. I hope they
>   like me... You know... Like, when
>   we meet.

Ivan is clearly uncomfortable with this topic and changes course.

>   IVAN
>   (Russian)
>   When will I meet your family?
>
>   ANI
>   (Russian)
>   Well, if you want to go to Miami...
>   my mom lives there with her man.
>   (beat) and you can meet my sister
>   anytime although I'm sure she'll
>   try to steal you... she's loves
>   Russian guys.

Ivan mimics her accent.

                    ANI (CONT'D)
          (English)
     Hey. I'm tryin' here. Asshole. Ok,
     English from now on for me.

                    IVAN
          (Russian)
     Your Russian is wonderful! It's
     great.

                    ANI
     You liar.

Ani playfully seduces him. She climbs on top of him and they start to fool around. Eventually they are having sex on the couch with her on top.

                              INTERCUT WITH:

INT. IGOR'S CAR - DAY

In Igor's 1983 Mercedes Diesel, Garnik and IGOR (early 30's, Russian) discuss the job as they are headed to the Zakharov mansion. They are both smoking.

                    GARNIK
          (Russian)
     Komsomolskaya Pravda ran a photo of
     him and some girl at a basketball
     game. And they are saying she's a
     prostitute.

Igor laughs. Garnik almost breaks but stops himself.

                    GARNIK (CONT'D)
          (Russian)
     It's not funny, man. Don't laugh.
     If it's true, Toros and I are
     fucked. Well, I'm not as fucked as
     Toros but still.

                    IGOR
          (Russian)
     Sounds like tabloid bullshit.

                    GARNIK
          (Russian)
     Probably. But look... if things get
     crazy, don't get rough with Ivan.
     Actually, don't even touch Ivan.
     Let me deal with him.

46.

> IGOR
> (Russian)
> What do you need me for then?

> GARNIK
> (Russian)
> In case his boys are here... and they want to play games.

They arrive at the front gate. Igor opens the driver's side window. Garnik leans over Igor and addresses the security guard.

> GARNIK (CONT'D)
> Hey. Is Ivan home?

> DAY GUARD
> He hasn't left while I've been here but my shift just started.

> GARNIK
> Do you know if he got married?

> DAY GUARD
> I just started my shift. I don't know...

> GARNIK
> Open the gate.

The gate opens and Igor drives on to the property.

INT. MANSION - DRIVEWAY - DAY

Garnik and Igor exit their car and walk toward the house. It's a cold winter day and their breath is visible. The men arrive at the door. They ring the doorbell.

INT. MANSION - LIVING ROOM - DAY

Ani and Ivan are startled mid-humping.

Ani crawls off of him.

> ANI
> Expecting guests?

Ivan motions to her to keep quiet. Ani is confused. Ivan gets up, pulls up his basketball shorts and tip-toes over to the door. Ani pulls up her panties. He looks through the windows to the side of the door. He recognizes Garnik. He has a silent freak out.

                    ANI (CONT'D)
                (mouthing)
            What?

The men see Ivan standing there with nothing but his shorts which tents a boner. Igor chuckles at the sight. Garnik is not amused.

                    IVAN
                (Russian)
            What? What do you want?

                    GARNIK
                (Russian)
            Ivan, we have to talk.

                    IVAN
                (Russian)
            Go away guys. I'm busy.

Garnik tries to talk to Ivan through the glass, projecting his voice.

                    GARNIK
                (Russian)
            Please Ivan, we have to talk.

                    IVAN
                (Russian)
            No. I have a guest.

Ani's eyebrows raise at the word guest.

                    GARNIK
                (Russian)
            Ivan, please.

                    IVAN
                (Russian)
            Not today. Goodbye! Go away.

Ivan shoos them away with his hand and begins to walk towards Ani who is now concerned.

                    ANI
            Who's that?

                    IVAN
                (Russian)
            Nobody, baby.

EXT. MANSION - FRONT STEPS - DAY

          GARNIK
    (Russian)
Son of a bitch.

Garnik takes out the key card and touches the pad, opening the door.

INT. MANSION - DOORWAY - DAY

Ivan realizes the door is opening and quickly runs towards the door and tries to push it back closed. Garnik sees this and thrusts his foot in the door jam to stop it from closing entirely.

          IVAN
    (Russian)
Hey! You can't just enter my home.

          GARNIK
    (Russian)
Ivan, please open the door.

          IVAN
    (Russian)
Fuck you, Garnik. I don't have to listen to you.

Ivan is pushing hard against the door.

          GARNIK
    (Russian)
That hurts my foot. Please stop that.

          IVAN
    (Russian)
Fuck you.

          GARNIK
    (Russian)
Ivan, your father sent us.

          IVAN
    (Russian)
My father sent you?

          GARNIK
    (Russian)
Well, not me. Your father sent Toros and Toros sent us.

                    IVAN
               (Russian)
          Where's Toros?

                    GARNIK
               (Russian)
          He's busy and he's very upset with
          you... if this is true.

                    IVAN
               (Russian)
          If what's true?

                    GARNIK
               (Russian)
          Did you get married to some
          prostitute?

                    ANI
          What did he say?

Garnik peeks around the crack of the door and sees Ani on the
couch.

                    GARNIK
               (Russian, to Ivan)
          Are you married? To her?

                    IVAN
               (Russian)
          Yes! Ok? Bye.

                    GARNIK
               (Russian)
          So you and her are married?

                    IVAN
               (Russian)
          Yes. I'm married.

                    GARNIK
               (Russian)
          Like officially with a license?

                    IVAN
               (Russian)
          Yes, officially. Goodbye!

                    GARNIK
               (Russian)
          You're in a lot of trouble.

Ivan tries to push Garnik's foot out of the way and
forcefully starts to close the door.

                    GARNIK (CONT'D)
                (Russian)
            Wait. Wait. I need to see the
            marriage license.

Ivan can't believe the request. Garnik follows that up with a
gentler approach.

                    GARNIK (CONT'D)
                (Russian)
            Now c'mon the faster we do it, the
            faster we're out of here.

                    IVAN
                (Russian)
            You've got to be kidding me. My
            parents are fucking crazy!
            Pathetic. Ok, they want proof. We
            give them proof.

Ivan stops pushing the door. The guys enter.

                    IVAN (CONT'D)
                (Russian, to Ani)
            Where's the marriage license?

Ani is very confused. Igor gives her the once over. Ani
catches him doing it.

                    IVAN (CONT'D)
                (English)
            The marriage license.

                    ANI
            It's in the desk. In the office.
            What's going on?

Ivan starts marching toward the elevator off the kitchen.

                    IVAN
                (Russian)
            Nothing. My parents are just being
            assholes.

                    ANI
            Who are these guys?

                    IVAN
                (Russian)
            My father's monkeys.

The elevator opens and Ivan and Garnik step in.

EXT. MANSION - DAY

We watch the elevator take Ivan and Garnik to the 3rd floor.

Ivan is fuming and throwing insults at Garnik.

INT. MANSION - LIVING ROOM - CONTINUOUS

Ani sits on the couch not knowing what to think. Igor nods politely at Ani. Ani is very uncomfortable.

          ANI
What's going on here?

          IGOR
I don't know.

          ANI
What are you doing here, that's what I'm asking.

          IGOR
I really don't know.

Ani is frustrated.

          IGOR (CONT'D)
I'm Igor.

Ani has no interest in conversing with him.

          ANI
I'm Ivan's wife.

INT. MANSION - 3RD FLOOR - CONTINUOUS

Ivan and Garnik exit the elevator and walk down the hall to the office.

INT. MANSION - OFFICE - CONTINUOUS

Ivan enters the office and walks over to the desk, opens the drawer and lifts up the marriage license.

          IVAN
          (Russian)
Look. See?

          GARNIK
          (Russian)
Let me see that.

Ivan hands him the marriage license. Garnik takes out his phone.

>   IVAN
>   (Russian)
>   What are you doing?

>   GARNIK
>   (Russian)
>   I've been asked to take a photo of
>   the license.

>   IVAN
>   (Russian)
>   My parents asked for a photo?

>   GARNIK
>   (Russian)
>   Toros.

>   IVAN
>   (Russian)
>   Oh my god. You people are pathetic.

Garnik takes a photo of the license and hands it back to Ivan.

>   IVAN (CONT'D)
>   (Russian)
>   Ok, on your way.

Garnik proceeds to text the photo.

                                                  CUT TO:

INT. ARMENIAN CHURCH - NAVE/ALTAR - DAY

The baptism ceremony has begun. Toros is standing at the altar holding the child. Toro's wife stands next to him. He feels the vibrating phone in his pocket. He can't resist and reaches down with one hand to check his phone. It's obvious he is not happy with what he's seeing.

>   TOROS
>   No!!!

The whole church reacts.

>   TOROS (CONT'D)
>   Excuse me, Father.

The priest continues the ceremony. Toros attempts to text back.

INT. MANSION - LIVING ROOM - DAY

Ivan and Garnik exit the elevator and enter the living room. Garnik is watching his phone.

>ANI

Is everything ok?

>IVAN

Yes.

>ANI

What's going on?

Ivan is leading Garnik and Igor toward the front door.

>IVAN
>(Russian)

Time to say goodbye. My wife and I would like some privacy, thank you. And tell Toros to go fuck himself.

>GARNIK
>(Russian)

Hold on.

>IVAN
>(Russian)

What do you mean? Leave.

>GARNIK
>(Russian)

I need to see what Toros says.

>IVAN
>(Russian)

What? C'mon. Enough is enough. Out.

Ding! Incoming text. Garnik reads the text.

>GARNIK

Standby.

>IVAN

Standby?
>(Russian)
What the fuck does that mean?

>GARNIK
>(Russian)

He wrote,
>(English)
'stand by'. So we stand by.

                    IVAN
          Stand by outside, man.

                    GARNIK
               (Russian)
          Ivan, with all due respect... your
          father sent us over.

                    IVAN
               (Russian)
          Toros sent you over.

                                        CUT TO:

INT. ARMENIAN CHURCH - ALTAR - DAY

Toros can't take it anymore.

                    TOROS
               (to priest)
          Father, I'm sorry.

Toros hands the child to his wife.

                    TOROS (CONT'D)
          Here. I'll be right back.

Toros exits the nave into the backroom. Everyone is confused.
Toros' wife looks appalled.

INT. ARMENIAN CHURCH - BACKROOM - DAY

Toros runs into the backroom of the church. He dials and puts
the phone to his ear. After a few seconds...

                    TOROS
               (Russian)
          Hello sir. Hello ma'am. So yes,
          apparently it is true.

Toros pulls the phone away from his ear, the screams are so
loud.

                                        CUT TO:

INT. MANSION - LIVING ROOM - DAY

Tensions are escalating.

                    ANI
          Hey... you guys work for Ivan's
          family... so I'm thinking that
          means you work for him. He told you
          to take it outside. Now, take it
          outside.

                                        CUT TO:

INT. ARMENIAN CHURCH - BACKROOM - DAY

Toros' phone call continues.

                    TOROS
               (Russian)
          I've seen the marriage license.

Screams come from the other side and once again Toros has to
pull the phone away from his ear.

                    TOROS (CONT'D)
               (Russian)
          Oh, I can't. I'm not with him. I'm
          actually not there. Garnik is. But
          I'm going over there right now to
          fix this. It will be fixed. Do not
          worry.

Toros listens to the angry Zakharovs on the other end for a
moment.

                    TOROS (CONT'D)
               (Russian)
          Oh no. That's not necessary.
          Really. You don't have to... I can
          handle this. Ok, ok. Got it. Yes
          sir. And yes, ma'am.

INT. MANSION - DOORWAY/FOYER - DAY

Garnik and Igor are being pushed out the door by Ivan. Igor
is doing as asked and completely complying. Ani is standing,
arms crossed. Garnik is delaying as politely as possible.

                    IVAN
               (Russian)
          Get out now or I'll have my father
          fire your fucking ass!

INT. ARMENIAN CHURCH - NAVE - DAY

Toros storms out of the backroom wearing his winter coat. He doesn't stop walking but addresses the parents and priest.

                    TOROS
          I'm so sorry I must go. There's an
          emergency.

Everyone is in shock. He turns to his wife.

                    TOROS (CONT'D)
          Ivan.

                    TOROS'S WIFE
              (Russian)
          Are you kidding me?

INT. MANSION - DOORWAY/FOYER - DAY

Finally saved by the ring tone. Garnik looks and shows them that Toros is calling.

                    GARNIK
          It's Toros.

He answers.

EXT. ARMENIAN CHURCH - FRONT STEPS - DAY

Toros storms out of the church. He screams into his phone.

                    TOROS
          Put me on speaker so the hooker can
          hear as well!

INT. MANSION - FOYER - DAY

                    ANI
          What the fuck! I'm not a fuckin'
          hooker!

                    IVAN
          She's not a hooker, she's an erotic
          dancer!

                    GARNIK
              (Armenian)
          You're already on speaker.

Igor is slightly amused by the chaos. Ani is confused, upset and starting to get angry. Toros (on speaker) proceeds to lay into Ivan (in Russian). He tells him how irresponsible he is and how much he screwed him after allowing him so much freedom while in America. Garnik awkwardly holds the phone for everyone to hear.

> TOROS
> (Russian)
> I don't check in on you in two weeks and you marry a whore?!?

> ANI
> I'm not a fucking whore you fucking Russian piece of shit.

> IVAN
> (Russian)
> They're Armenian.

> ANI
> You Armenian piece of shit!

EXT. CHURCH - PARKING LOT - CONTINUOUS

While screaming into his phone, he jumps into his WHITE ESCALADE and tears out of the parking lot. The call goes through his car radio speakers.

INT / EXT ESCALADE & MANSION FOYER - CONTINUOUS

We intercut between the escalade (87.1) and the mansion (87.2).

> TOROS
> (Russian)
> Well guess what? You really did it this time. Ready? Ready? YOUR PARENTS ARE ON THEIR WAY!

> IVAN
> (Russian)
> WHAT!?!?

> TOROS
> (Russian)
> Yes. Like a school boy, you're being picked up by your parents because you were naughty. We're meeting them tomorrow at noon.

                    IVAN
          NOOOO!

                    TOROS
          And taking your ass back to St.
          Petersburg, so start packing.

                    IVAN
          FUCK!!!!

Garnik feels like he's being screamed at so he places the
phone down on the counter and steps back.

                    ANI
               (to Ivan)
          We're married, baby. They have to
          accept that.

Ivan can't handle this news. This is all new to Igor who
silently is amused by the twists and turns he is hearing.

                    TOROS
          Accept that? That's funny. Ok.
               (Russian)
          Ivan, I'll be there in ten minutes
          and you and the streetwalker are
          coming with me...

                    ANI
          Did he just say streetwalker?

                    TOROS
               (Russian)
          ...down to city hall where we're
          getting this marriage annulled.

                    ANI
          What? What does that mean?

                    TOROS
          We are going down to city hall
          where this fake marriage will be
          annulled. Canceled. So be ready to
          go by the time I get there. And
          missy... you're out of that house
          TONIGHT!

It strikes Ani at that moment that her new life could be
taken away in a flash.

                    ANI
          I'm not going anywhere you, fucking
          piece of shit.
               (MORE)

58.

                    ANT (CONT'D)
          We're not getting divorced because
          you tell us to. Go fuck yourself!
          Right Ivan?

                    IVAN
               (Russian)
          My parents are coming?

                    TOROS
               (Russian)
          Yes, you little shit. They are
          leaving Russia now.

Ivan is silent.

                    TOROS (CONT'D)
               (English)
          You hear me?

Finally...

                    IVAN
               (Russian)
          Well, I'm out of here so fuck you.

Ivan turns to Ani. Ivan grabs his jeans and tee shirt and throws them on.

                    IVAN (CONT'D)
               (Russian)
          C'mon, get dressed. We're going.

                    ANI
          Wait what?

                    GARNIK
               (Russian)
          No, Ivan. You can't leave.

Ivan opens the closet near the front door, grabs his jacket and sneakers. The closet door remains open.

                    IVAN
               (Russian)
          The fuck I can't. (English to Ani)
          Let's go!

                    ANI
          Going where? What? What's going on?

                                                  CUT TO:

INT. TOROS' ESCALADE - DAY

Toros is racing down the street while hearing all of this commotion through his speaker.

            TOROS
    Wait. Did he say he was leaving?
    No! Don't let him leave.

INT. MANSION - LIVING ROOM/FOYER - DAY

Ivan is grabs his phone.

            ANI
    Ivan, why do we have to leave our
    house?

            IVAN
    Let's go, let's go, let's go.

            ANI
    Let me get dressed. Ivan, what's
    happening?

She suddenly realizes he is about to leave. Igor steps forward and blocks her way. Garnik is doing everything he can to diffuse the situation.

            IVAN
    Ok, Bye.

Ivan hits the GATE button on the console. Ivan exits.

            ANI
    Ivan! Wait! Are you fucking kidding
    me?

                                        CUT TO:

INT. TOROS' ESCALADE - DAY

On speakerphone and driving, Toros is freaking out. It's all out of his control.

            TOROS
    Did he say bye? NOOOO! Get him!
    What's happening!

                                        CUT TO:

INT. MANSION - FOYER - DAY

                    GARNIK
          (Russian, pointing to Ani)
     Keep her here.

Garnik runs after Ivan. Ani moves toward the door. Igor blocks her way.

                    IGOR
          (to Ani)
     Please sit down.

                    ANI
     Get out of my way.

                    IGOR
     Please.

Igor grabs her shoulder to stop her.

                    ANI
     Get your hands off me.

                    IGOR
     Calm down.

                    ANI
     Don't fucking touch me.

Igor points to the couch and begins to push her toward it. Ani sees red and swings at Igor.

INT. MANSION - DRIVEWAY - CONTINUOUS

Ivan runs through the open gate. Garnik is close behind but slips on an ice patch and goes down.

                    GARNIK
     Ivan!

INT. MANSION - FOYER/FAMILY ROOM - CONTINUOUS

Ani swings again. Igor is doing his best to keep his cool. This time she strikes with her left hand. The wedding ring breaks skin on Igor's cheek. First blood.

                    IGOR
          (Russian)
     Impressive.

Ani continues to back away as Igor approaches.

                    ANI
          Stay away from me!

She attempts to run to the side door and Igor runs to block
her from leaving. She grabs the menorah off the table behind
the couch and throws it at Igor. He ducks and the meorah hits
a painting on the wall, shattering the glass frame.

Ani runs around the couch but Igor leaps the couch and grabs
her. She screams bloody murder.

                                        CUT TO:

INT. TOROS' ESCALADE - DAY

Toros hears Ani's screaming through the speaker.

                    TOROS
          What's happening!

INT. MANSION - FAMILY ROOM - DAY

Ani is fighting hard. They fall against a side table that
causes a red lamp to topple and shatter across the marble
floor. Igor is doing his best to subdue Ani but she is
fighting back like a wild banshee. She frees one of her arms
and pounds away at Igor, hitting him in the side and neck.
Their bodies fall against another table, adorned with vases
and a candle holder, which all topple to the floor. The
landline phone remains on the table.

INT. TOROS' ESCALADE - DAY

Toros tears around a corner. He hears the screaming and
commotion.

                    TOROS
          Are you killing her? What's
          happening? Stop it!

EXT. MANSION/STREET - DAY

Outside the mansion, Garnik chases Ivan down the street. Ivan
is far ahead. Finally Garnik gives up on pursuing Ivan and
runs back. The security guard looks stumped.

                    DAY GUARD
          What's going on?

                    GARNIK
          Nothing.

                    DAY GUARD
          Everything ok?

                    GARNIK
          What?

                    DAY GUARD
          Everything ok?

                    GARNIK
          Yeah.

                    DAY GUARD
          Ivan having one of his tantrums?

Garnik is frazzled and doesn't reply. Trying to run, Garnik limps back toward the house. The guard is amused as if he's seen something like this before.

                    DAY GUARD (CONT'D)
          Fucking Russians.

INT. MANSION - FOYER/FAMILY ROOM - DAY

Igor gets her pinned on the couch, holding her hands down. It is nearly impossible because of how hard Ani is resisting. Ani screams and swears. Igor sees the landline phone within arm's reach and grabs it off the table. He pulls the phone and cord right off the base, flips Ani over and ties her wrists. Ani screams and struggles even more.

Garnik enters the front door.

                    GARNIK
              (Armenian)
          Oh my god.
              (Russian)
          What's happening?

                    IGOR
              (Russian)
          Help me. She's crazy.

                    GARNIK
              (Russian)
          What's happening?

                    IGOR
              (Russian)
          She's crazy. Come and help me
          please!

                    ANI
          Help me! He's attacking me.

                    GARNIK
              (Russian)
          What did you do to her?

                    IGOR
              (Russian)
          You want me to keep her from going
          or what?

                    GARNIK
              (Russian)
          Yes but...

                    IGOR
              (Russian)
          She's out of fucking control. Look!

He points to his bleeding face.

INT. TOROS' ESCALADE - DAY

                    TOROS
          Garnik! Garnik, you fucking idiot!

Toros is totally distracted by what he's hearing and is
screaming at the radio. He looks up and panics. He slams on
the brakes and comes to a screeching halt right in front of a
young child in the middle of the street. The child gives
Toros a WTF look.

                    TOROS (CONT'D)
          Jesus fucking christ.

The kid slowly moves out of the way and Toros drives off.

INT. MANSION - FAMILY ROOM - DAY

                    IGOR
              (Russian)
          I need your help. Grab that cord
          and tie her legs.

                    GARNIK
              (Russian)
          That cord?

                    IGOR
              (Russian)
          Yes, hurry man, that cord.

                    ANI
          You two are fucking dead for this.
          I'm Ivan's fucking wife.

Garnik grabs the cord from a shattered lamp that still has the lightbulb socket attached. He approaches Ani's feet reluctantly. Suddenly, she kicks him square in the face, breaking his nose. He falls back and crashes through the glass coffee table. Glass shatters everywhere.

Disoriented and in pain, Garnik stands and cups his face.

                    GARNIK *
          (Russian) She broke my fucking noce
          man. (English) You broke my nose
          you fucking bitch!

                    ANI
          Good. I'm glad I broke your fucking
          nose.

Garnik realizes his nose is bleeding and like a zombie walks towards the kitchen.

                    ANI (CONT'D)
          You two are fucking dead for this.
          I'm Ivan's fucking wife!

This echoes through the house.

INT. MANSION - KITCHEN - CONTINUOUS

Garnik stumbles into the kitchen and opens the freezer.

INT. MANSION - FAMILY ROOM - CONTINUOUS

                    ANI
          Let me the fuck go.

                    IGOR
          Please stop.

					ANI
			I'm not fighting you. I'm not going
			to run. You're fucking hurting me.
			Let me go.

					IGOR
			I can't.

INT. MANSION - KITCHEN - CONTINUOUS

Garnik can not find ice and takes a bag of frozen dumplings.

INT. MANSION - FAMILY ROOM - CONTINUOUS

Ani is exasperated.

					ANI
			I will make sure you go away for
			this. Look, there are cameras
			everywhere. You're so fucked.

Igor does not reply.

INT. TOROS' ESCALADE - DAY

Toros lays into the horn as he speeds down the Belt. He
pounds the steering wheel in frustration.

INT. MANSION - FAMILY ROOM - DAY

					ANI
			Just wait until Ivan sees what you
			did to me.

					IGOR
			The Ivan that just left you?

					ANI
			He didn't leave me. He went for
			help.

					IGOR
			I don't think so.

Garnik slowly walks into the family room. He grabs his phone
on the way.

					GARNIK
			Toros, we have a situation here
			man.

                    TOROS
            I'm pulling up now!

Garnik, dumpling bag to his face, sits on the couch across from them.

                    GARNIK
                (Russian)
            She broke my fucking nose, man. You
            broke my nose you fucking bitch!

EXT. MANSION - SECURITY GATE - DAY

Toros speeds up to the gate.

                    TOROS
            Open the gate!

                    GUARD
            Ok but sir...

                    TOROS
            Open this fucking gate now!

INT. MANSION - FAMILY ROOM - DAY

                    ANI
            Fucking piece of shit. I bet you
            like this, don't you. You getting
            off on this? Psycho fuck.

                    IGOR
            I don't like this. I'm not being
            paid enough for this.

                    ANI
            I can feel you getting hard
            motherfucker.

EXT. MANSION - DRIVEWAY - DAY

Toros exits the Escalade and darts to the front door. He scans his card and pushes open the door.

INT. MANSION - FIRST FLOOR - DAY

Toros enters the mansion.

                    ANI
            Vanya!

                    IGOR
          It's not Vanya.

Toros enters and cannot believe what he sees. The family room
is in shambles, shattered glass and ceramic, Garnik holding
the dumpling bag to his face, Igor bear hugging Ani on the
couch and no Ivan to speak of.

Total shock and awe. Toros can not believe it.

                    TOROS
          Oh my God. Oh my god. What? What is
          happening? Who did this?

                    GARNIK
          She did this!

                    ANI
          Hey! You the fuck on the phone?!?

Toros doesn't even hear Ani, he's in such shock.

                    TOROS
          What the happened? What the fuck
          happened?

                    GARNIK
          She happened!

                    ANI
          Yo! Boss man! I'm talking to you!
          What's happening? Tell this fuck to
          let me go!

                    TOROS
          (to Garnik) Did you touch Ivan?
          Where's Ivan?

                    GARNIK
          No, Ivan took off when you told him
          his parents are coming and this
          bitch freaks out. Fucking kicks me
          in the face, I think she broke my
          nose, man.

                    ANI
          That's not true! What the fuck is
          happening!!!!

                    TOROS
          What do you mean took off?

                    ANI
          Yo! Fuck face!

68.

GARNIK
He ran away.

TOROS
Ran away?

GARNIK
Yes! Ran away!

TOROS
On foot?

GARNIK
(Armenian) Yes, he ran away man.

ANI
They scared him!

TOROS
Oh my god.

GARNIK
I was trying to stop Ivan from leaving and...

TOROS
Trying? You just stop him from leaving. There's no trying. What are you talking about?

Toros takes his phone from his pocket and attempts to call Ivan.

GARNIK
(Armenian)
I can't touch the fucking guy. What are you talking about?

Toros looks at Igor.

IGOR
(Russian)
What? What did he say?

TOROS
(Russian)
Why did you let him leave?

IGOR
(Russian, referring to
Garnik then Ani)
He told me not to touch the guy. And I was dealing with her.

It goes to voicemail.

                    TOROS
          He's not answering. Let me think.
          Let me think.

He puts the phone back in his pocket. Finally Toros acknowledges Ani.

                    TOROS (CONT'D)
          Is this her?

                    ANI
          If you mean Ivan's wife? Yes! Tell
          him to let me go.

                    TOROS
          Where's Ivan!

                    ANI
          You tell me! Please, I'm not going
          to run. Tell him to let me go.

                    GARNIK
          No, don't let her go.

                    ANI
          Tell him!

                    TOROS
          Let her go!

                    GARNIK
          No, don't. She's an animal.

                    TOROS
          She's a girl. What are you talking
          about?

                    GARNIK
          She doesn't fight like one.

                    TOROS
          Let her go!

Igor finally releases her. He lifts Ani off and she sits to his left.

                    ANI
          Fuck! Now fucking untie me!

Toros sees the phone cord around her wrist.

                    TOROS
            Why is she tied? What is happening!

                    ANI
            That's what I want to know! What
            the fuck is happening!

                    TOROS
            Where's Ivan.

                    ANI
            I told you, I don't know. Please
            untie me.

                    TOROS
            Call him!

                    ANI
            Untie me!

                    TOROS
            Why is she tied up.

                    GARNIK
            Look!

Garnik points to his face. Toros looks over to Igor. Igor
pulls his collar to reveal the bite mark.

                    TOROS
            What, the two of you get beat up by
            a little girl?

                    ANI
            Untie me now, motherfucker. This is
            so fucking illegal!

                    GARNIK
            Don't do that!

Ani stands up.

                    ANI
            You fuck! Untie me now!

Igor jumps up and pulls her back down on the couch.

                    TOROS
            And c'mon. This is overkill. Untie
            her. Ridiculous.

                    IGOR
               (Russian)
          I don't suggest that. Get what you
          need first. She's not co-operative.

                    ANI
          Shut the fuck up.

                    GARNIK
          I'm leaving if you untie her!

                    TOROS
          I need you to call Ivan.

                    ANI
          Untie me and I'll call him.

                    TOROS
          Where's your phone.

                    ANI
          Untie me.

                    GARNIK
          Don't do it.

                    TOROS
          Call him and get him back here and
          then you'll be untied.

                    ANI
          Fuck you!

                    TOROS
          Where's your phone!

Ani turns away.

                    IGOR
          It's in the other room.

                    ANI
          Fuck!

                    TOROS
          Get it.

Igor gets up and walks to the living room. On the coffee table, lies Ani's phone - with the name Ani in rhinestones.

Toros paces the living room.

                    TOROS (CONT'D)
          We have until noon tomorrow morning
          to find this little prick and get
          you two split.

                    ANI
          Look. Your guy fucking attacked me.
          Both of them did. They forced their
          way in, fought with Ivan and then
          physically attacked me. What is
          going on?

                    TOROS
          I'm sorry it went down that way but
          it looks like they're the ones who
          were physically attacked. Now let's
          call Ivan and tell him to get back
          here.

Toros face ID's her and starts scrolling through contacts.

                    ANI
          It's under HUSBAND.

He calls and it goes to voicemail. This is another indication to Ani that Ivan does not care for her well-being.

                    TOROS
                (to Ani)
          Great husband you have here.
          Ditches you and now doesn't answer
          your calls. Yeah, this marriage is
          real, my ass.

                    ANI
          Look, I don't know what kind of
          family drama is going on here but
          Ivan and I are married. It's a real
          marriage and I'm not getting
          divorced.

                    TOROS
          The marriage isn't real and we are
          getting it annulled and you have no
          say in it. So let bygones be
          bygones and let's go find Ivan and
          get this fixed.

                    ANI
          I'm his wife. I think I have a say
          in it.

TOROS
Look. You two got married
illegally. It's a fraud marriage
and we are getting it annulled
right now.

ANI
We are two consenting adults who
are legally married and there's
nothing you can do about it.

TOROS
(shouting)
This is just Ivan playing around!
Get over it!

ANI
No it's not, you have no idea.

TOROS
Oh yeah, how long have you known
Ivan? When did you meet?

Ani doesn't reply.

TOROS (CONT'D)
You don't know this guy.

ANI
I know my husband.

TOROS
No you don't. He took you for a
ride, lady. This is classic Ivan.
(beat)
Little bastard. I've been dealing
with his shit since he was six-
years-old. Now his parents are
going to kill me and my fucking
family will never speak to me
again. This little prick!

ANI
I love my husband and I plan on
being with him forever.

TOROS
You are not in love and neither is
he.

ANI
(seething)
I can't wait to have Ivan's children. I'm probably already pregnant.

TOROS
I hope you're not because we'll be taking care of that as well if you are.

ANI
The fuck you will.

TOROS
Hey! Ivan doesn't love you. He just hates his parents. Now let's go find Ivan and get this taken care of.

ANI
Ivan won't divorce me.

TOROS
Ha! He shamed his family, marrying somebody like you. And if you think for a minute this will be allowed to continue, you're dead wrong.

ANI
I'm staying married.

TOROS
We're getting this annulled now.

ANI
The fuck we are. And I would like you to leave my home now. Or I'll be pressing charges.

Toros laughs.

TOROS
This isn't Ivan's house. This is his father's. You're technically trespassing.

ANI
I'm married to Ivan and this is our home!

                    TOROS
          You married Ivan, not his father.
          Everything in here is Ivan's
          father's. The money belongs to his
          father. Ivan has nothing. (beat)
          The bedroom you two have been
          fucking in... that's his parent's
          room. His is down the hall... the
          one with the spaceships on the
          wall... cause he's a fucking child!

Toros leans into her.

                    TOROS (CONT'D)
               (very serious)
          Look, the son of Nikolai Zakharov
          is not marrying a whore.

Ani doesn't reply.

                    TOROS (CONT'D)
          Rich marry rich. That's the way it
          works. Not this.
               (beat)
          You help fix this or you're going
          to be arrested.

                    ANI
          Me arrested!?
               (shouting)
          You should be fucking arrested!

                    TOROS
               (pointing to the scarf)
          What did I say?

Ani lowers her voice.

                    ANI
          Arrest me for what?!

                    TOROS
          Fraud, trespassing, extortion,
          theft.

                    ANI
          What?!?! Theft?

                    TOROS
          Yes, you married Ivan to steal from
          his family.

                    ANI
          I'm sorry... what?

                    TOROS
          You heard me. I think it's pretty
          clear that Ivan was taken advantage
          of by a...
               (making it up as he goes
                along)
          scheming... prostitute... because
          of his family's wealth.

                    ANI
          What?

                    TOROS
          And I'm sure you already have a
          criminal record so...

                    ANI
          Fuck you. He proposed to me. He
          wanted to get married. Look, he
          bought me a 4 carat diamond wedding
          ring.

Ani rolls to her side to show him the ring.

                    TOROS
          Give me that.

                    ANI
          NOOOOOO!

Toros gestures to Igor to help him take her ring off. Ani
screams bloody murder. Finally they succeed in removing the
ring.

                    TOROS
          This is the property of the
          Zakharov's.

Igor clocks Toros putting the ring in his jacket pocket.

                    ANI
          RAPE!

The men are perplexed.

                    ANI (CONT'D)
          RAPE!

The men panic.

							TOROS
					What is she saying? Rape? What
					rape?

Ani continues to scream.

							TOROS (CONT'D)
					Shut up! Shut up! Shut her up.

							ANI
					Help! Rape! Rape! Help!

Toros covers her mouth with his hand. She bites and he pulls it away.

							IGOR
					She's a biter. If you want her to
					shut up, you need to gag her.

							TOROS
					We have to shut her up. The guard
					will hear!

Toros runs to the closet in the foyer and grabs a designer red scarf.

										CUT TO:

EXT. MANSION - PATIO - MOMENTS LATER

Toros is smoking a cigarette and talking on his cell while Garnik is spitting blood onto the snow bank in the backyard.

							TOROS
					Oh, don't give me that shit.
					They're landing at noon. You get us
					in front of the judge first thing
					or the family will be cutting ties
					with the firm tomorrow. Simple as
					that.

										CUT TO:

INT. MANSION - FAMILY ROOM - DAY

Ani sits bound and gagged on the couch. Igor stands between her and the front door with his arms crossed.

                    IGOR
          I'm sorry I had to do that but you
          gave me no choice.

Ani turns and stares him down.

                    IGOR (CONT'D)
          Just do what they say. It'll be so
          much easier.

                                             CUT TO:

EXT. MANSION - PATIO - DAY

                    TOROS
          We'll see you at 9. Yeah, I have
          it.
               (beat)
          Yes. Ok.

Toros hangs up and looks through the glass at Ani on the couch.

                    TOROS (CONT'D)
               (Armenian)
          Ok, time to break this broad.

He chucks the butt and heads inside.

INT. MANSION - FAMILY ROOM - MOMENTS LATER

Igor removes the gag. The men stand over Ani. Ani looks up at the three men with pure hatred in her eyes.

                    TOROS
          Ok? Calm now? Going to behave?

Ani just stares.

                    TOROS (CONT'D)
          Trust me. I know. I know what
          you're thinking.

                    TOROS (CONT'D)
          You're thinking that this little
          shit betrayed you. I know how you
          feel because he's betrayed me too.

                    GARNIK
          Me too.

                    TOROS
          He's betrayed all of us. And most
          importantly, he betrayed his family
          by marrying you. He's a spoiled
          brat who doesn't want to grow up.
          And he pushed it too far this time.
          But I want to help you. The way I
          see it... this was a green card
          marriage and therefore Ivan owes
          you a green card marriage fee.
          That's only fair. We get this
          annulled and I will see to it that
          you get a 10K fee, good?

Toros moves forward to take off her gag.

                    TOROS (CONT'D)
          No screaming ok? You scream and the
          gag goes back on.

She nods and he takes the gag off.

                    TOROS (CONT'D)
          10K. That's as good as you're going
          to get honey.

                    ANI
             (long beat)
          I want to talk to Ivan before
          agreeing to this.

                    TOROS
          We want to talk to Ivan too. So we
          want the same thing.

After a long beat...

                    ANI
          So let's find Ivan.

                    TOROS
          Ok, but look at me. When we find
          Ivan, which we will. And we get
          this marriage annulled, which we
          will. You walk away with 10K and
          never contact Ivan again. Yes?

Another long beat...

                    ANI
          Sure.

                              TOROS
                    Ok, untie her.
                         (turning to Garnik)
                    The license and his passport.

INT. MANSION - MASTER BEDROOM - DAY

Ani removes her lashes from her eyes, washes her face and
opens the bathroom door. Igor is waiting outside the door.

                              ANI
                    Excuse me. I would like some
                    privacy while I change.

EXT. MANSION - FRONT STEPS/DRIVEWAY - DAY

Ani and the guys exit the house, walk down the front steps
and across the driveway to the Escalade. Ani wears the black
sable coat. Toros is shoving the passports in his inside
pocket as he looks over the license.

                              TOROS
                    Anora Mikheyova?

                              ANI
                    Ani, it's Ani.

                              TOROS
                    It says Anora.

                              ANI
                    I know. But I go by Ani, thank you!

Igor is clearly listening to this exchange. In the
background, a mid size car with Klara and her co-workers
enter the open gate.

EXT. MANSION/INT. TOROS' ESCALADE - DAY - CONTINUOUS

Igor opens the back seat door for Ani. She gets in. Toros
snaps and points to the back. Igor gets in the backseat with
Ani.

                              ANI
                    Why is he getting back here with
                    me? I don't want this fucking
                    psychopath back here with me.

				GARNIK
		Because I'm not sitting back there
		with you. You're the fucking
		psychopath!

Klara and her two co-workers are walking toward the house.
They carry cleaning supplies. They pass the escalade as Toros
is backing out. Toros opens the window.

				TOROS
		You have a big mess to clean in
		there.

He reaches in his jacket and pulls out a $100 bill and hands
it to Klara.

				TOROS (CONT'D)
		Here. No questions.

OMITTED

INT. TOROS' ESCALADE - DAY

				TOROS
		He hangs there?

				ANI
		Yeah and his friends own it or
		manage it or some shit.

				TOROS
		And he'll be there?

				ANI
		I have no fucking idea.

				TOROS
		Ok, he better be there.

				GARNIK
		I have to go to the hospital, man.

				TOROS
		No, you don't. You're fine. We find
		Ivan and then... my wife will patch
		you up. She's good at that.

				GARNIK
			(Armenian)
		I think I have a concussion, man.

The two continue to argue about going to the hospital. In the backseat, Igor turns to Ani.

>   IGOR
>   Sorry for what happened back there.
>   It didn't have to be that
>   difficult.

Ani turns and glares and then turns forward.

>   ANI
>   I don't want him talking to me.

>   TOROS
>   (Russian) Leave her alone man.

Garnik begins complaining again.

>   IGOR
>   (Russian)
>   Swing by my place. I have something
>   for him.

>   TOROS
>   Goddamn it!

EXT. BRIGHTWATER - DAY

They are parked in front. Igor exits the building, enters the car. He hands three pills up to Garnik who pops them in his mouth. Igor is taken aback to see him take all three at once.

>   TOROS
>   Ok? Good? Let's go.

Toros drives off.

EXT. WEST 10TH ST. - DAY

The escalade pulls on to 10th St.

>   TOROS
>   The hell is this?

The car can't pull any further forward due to the street being closed and blocked by two concrete NYPD barricades. Toros throws it in to park.

>   TOROS (CONT'D)
>   Ok, out. Let's go.

The crew exits the parked Escalade. Toros looks back and locks the car with his key.

                    IGOR
          (Russian) Car is ok there?

                    TOROS
          It's fine. Let's go.

The crew walks down 10th Street past the CYCLONE rollercoaster.

OMITTED

EXT. CONEY ISLAND BOARDWALK - DAY

They walk up onto the boardwalk and take a right... walking down to the Vape Shop.

INT. VAPE SHOP - DAY

The crew enter the small shop. Crystal and Tom are behind the counter. They can tell something is up.

                    CRYSTAL
          Hey Ani.

                    ANI
          Hey guys. Have you guys seen Ivan?

Crystal and Tom look at each other. Tom shakes his head.

                    CRYSTAL
          Not today.

                    TOROS
          You talk to him today?

                    TOM
          Who are you?

                    TOROS
          I asked you a question.

                    TOM
          And I asked you a question.

                    TOROS
          Look, Ivan's in a lot of trouble.
          We need to find him. We need to
          know if you talked with him?

                    TOM
          And I'll ask you again... who the
          fuck are you?

Toros is triggered. Igor can tell this may get ugly. Ani
jumps in.

                    ANI
          Can you call Ivan for me?

                    CRYSTAL
          And why can't you call him?

                    ANI
          Just... can you do me a favor and
          call him?

                    CRYSTAL
          Actually I find this peculiar.
               (beat)
          Who are these guys and why are you
          asking other people to call your
          husband for you?

                    ANI
          Crystal, we have a problem and I
          need to find Ivan.

Crystal looks at Tom.

                    CRYSTAL
          What's the problem?

                    TOROS
          Enough. One of you call Ivan, now.

                    TOM
          This isn't our business man. We
          haven't seen him so...

Tom motions for them to leave the shop.

                    TOM (CONT'D)
          ...Thank you.

                    TOROS
          If you aided him in this fraud of a
          marriage, then it is your business.

Ani's heart drops. Garnik steps in.

                    GARNIK
         One of you better get Ivan on the
         line now.

Crystal and Tom laugh at Garnik.

                    TOM
         What does 'on the line' mean, you
         old fuck.

                    TOROS
         One of you call Ivan now.

Again they refuse.

Toros has had enough and walks towards the counter aggressively.

                    TOROS (CONT'D)
         Give me your phone, you little
         fuck.

Tom takes out a golf club.

                    TOM
         I don't think so.

Tom comes out from behind the counter holding the golf club. The crew begins to back up.

                    TOM (CONT'D)
         Leave. Now. C'mon. Out.

Igor does not like being threatened and moves slowly. Tom pokes Igor to get him out the door. Not a good move. Igor stops, turns and looks at Tom.

                    IGOR
         What are you planning to do with
         that?

                    TOM
         I'm planning out beating your ass
         if you don't get out now.

Suddenly, Igor snatches the golf club out of Tom's hand.

                    IGOR
         Now what?

                    TOROS
          Call Ivan now or my friend here is
          going to practice his stroke on
          your fucking face.

                    TOM
          Fuck you.

Igor looks at Toros who gives an approving nod. Igor swings
the club down through the glass shelves on his right. They
explode and shatter numerous glass bongs in the process.

Tom and Crystal scream for him to stop. He turns and smashes
the top of the glass counter.

                    CRYSTAL
          Stop! Tell him to stop!

Ani looks at Crystal.

                    ANI
          Fucking call Ivan. NOW!

Shaking, Crystal calls Ivan.

Ani grabs the phone.

                    TOROS
          Speaker.

Ani hits the speaker button. They hear it goes to voicemail.
Ani drops the phone. Toros spins to Tom.

                    TOROS (CONT'D)
          You. Call him now.

Tom starts to call him.

                    TOROS (CONT'D)
          Speaker.

It goes to voicemail. We hear Ivan's obnoxious greeting
again.

                    TOROS (CONT'D)
          Where are his other friends?

Ani looks at Crystal.

                    ANI
          Is he with Aleks?

CRYSTAL
(in tears)
I told you. I don't know.

Tom struggles on the floor in pain.

TOM
He can't be with Aleks! Aleks is at work.

TOROS
Where does he work?

Crystal looks to her brother for approval. Tom shrugs.

CRYSTAL
Tatiana's.

TOROS
Ok, let's go.

The crew files out of the shop.

HARD CUT TO:

EXT. BOARDWALK - MOMENTS LATER

They walk out onto the boardwalk. Igor is still winding down from the confrontation and Ani is obviously very upset about being hung up on. Ani steels herself against the cold wind with the sable.

TOROS
Ok, let's go.

ANI
We're walking!?!

GARNIK
Why don't we drive?

IGOR
(Russian)
That's a 10 minute walk.

Toros starts walking.

TOROS
It's faster if we walk. I'm not finding parking again.

Ani, Igor and Garnik huff and puff as they follow Toros. We track with the four down the boardwalk. They all smoke.

EXT. TATIANA'S GRILL - DAY

The sea themed and more low-key sister of the famed TATIANA'S GRILL, a Brighton Beach staple. The crew arrives.

INT. TATIANA'S GRILL - DAY

The crew enter and are greeted by a HOSTESS.

          HOSTESS
Table for four?

          TOROS
Where's Aleks?

          HOSTESS
Aleks?

They look around the main room where an affable SINGER performs and patrons enjoy the music. Ani points toward the kitchen.

          ANI
There he is.

They storm the kitchen causing a scene.

INT. TATIANA'S GRILL - KITCHEN - DAY - CONTINUOUS

Aleks is startled to see the crew charging into the kitchen.

          ALEKS
What's going on?

          ANI
Have you seen Ivan?

          ALEKS
No, what's going on?

          TOROS
You talk with him? You know where he is?

          ALEKS
The fuck is going on?

Aleks is confused and overwhelmed. His co-workers back away from the building chaos.

                    ANI
          We have an emergency. We need to
          find Ivan.

                    ALEKS
          I haven't seen him today.

                    TOROS
          Call him.

                    ALEKS
          Call him?

                    TOROS
          You heard me. Call him.

Aleks takes out his phone and calls Ivan. Toros snatches the
phone out of Aleks's hand. He listens. Goes to voicemail.

                    TOROS (CONT'D)
          Fuck. He knows we're looking for
          him.

                    ALEKS
          Can I have my phone back please.

                    TOROS
          Where can I find Ivan?

                    ALEKS
          He's probably at home. I don't
          fucking know.

                    ANI
          He's not there. And Tom and Crystal
          haven't seen him.

Toros is about to explode. He looks into the main section of
the restaurant and has an idea.

                    ALEKS
          Yeah well, I don't know either so
          can you guys please... you going to
          cost me my job here.

Toros turns to Ani.

                    TOROS
          I need a photo of Ivan.

Ani shrugs.

                    TOROS (CONT'D)
          C'mon, you must have a photo of the
          man you married.

                    ANI
          You're not taking my phone again.

                    TOROS
          Give me your fucking phone!

                    ANI
          I will fucking scream if you touch
          me.

                    IGOR
          Use his Instagram.

                    TOROS
          I don't have Instagram. I'm an
          adult.

                    GARNIK
          Here.

Garnik, opens his phone and passes it to Toros. Garnik looks at Ivan's Instagram account.

                    TOROS
          If we looked at his fucking
          Instagram we would have known this
          shit two weeks ago.

He choses the first photo. It's a photo of Ani and Ivan. He zooms past Ani to enlarge Ivan's face. He storms out of the kitchen into the main room.

INT. TATIANA'S GRILL - MAIN AREA - CONTINUOUS

He swiftly walks across the room and grabs the mic out of the performer's hands.

                    TOROS
          Everybody. Listen up.

Everything Toros says, he repeats in Russian.

                    TOROS (CONT'D)
          I need everybody to take a look at
          this photo. We have a missing
          person and we need help now. Has
          anybody seen this kid?

91.

Toros proceeds to walk around the room, showing the customers the silly photo of Ivan, disrupting everybody's Sunday dinner. Nobody has seen him.

INT. TATIANA'S GRILL - KITCHEN - CONTINUOUS

ALEKS
The fuck is going on?

ANI
Could he be with Dasha?

ALEKS
Pfft. Not unless he's in the Bahamas with her and her new fuck boy.

ANI
Fuck.

ALEKS
Yeah, she left my ass the minute we got back from Vegas. And you know why? 'Cause she said I'd never propose to her the way Ivan proposed to you. Can you believe that shit? And the thing is... I would. I would have. I'm actually like a romantic, you know.

Ani is not listening.

EXT. BOARDWALK - LATE AFTERNOON

They exit Tatiana's.

TOROS
Goddamn it!

A strong gust of cold wind blows in from the beach. The crew cringes.

TOROS (CONT'D)
Ok, well, let's go. No time to waste.

ANI
What? All the way back?

					GARNIK
				(Armenia)
			This is why we should have driven
			man. My fucking head is going to
			explode.

					TOROS
			The cold is good for that, c'mon.

					ANI
			I'm not walking the whole way back.
			You can get the car and pick us up.

					TOROS
			The hell I am. It'll be dark soon.
			Move.

Toros leads the crew down the boardwalk.

EXT. BRIGHTON BEACH/CONEY ISLAND BOARDWALK - MINUTES LATER

The crew march through the cold. Ani is shivering. Igor reaches into his pocket and pulls out the red scarf from earlier.

					IGOR
				(to Ani)
			Hey.

Ani is startled when she sees him holding the red scarf towards her.

She stops walking.

					ANI
			The fuck?

					IGOR
			Here. This will help.
				(Russian)
			You'll get a nasty cold if you
			don't cover your neck.

					ANI
			Why do you have that with you?

					IGOR
			What?

					ANI
			Why did you bring that with you?

Igor looks down at the scarf and realizes he shouldn't answer that question.

              ANI (CONT'D)
      In case you had to gag me again
      motherfucker?

Igor has no words.

              ANI (CONT'D)
      Yeah, that's what I thought. Fuck
      you, you piece of shit.
      Unfuckingbelievable.

Ani storms ahead. Igor trails behind. They all walk in silence for a while. Quite a while. The wind is strong and cold. Finally...

              ANI (CONT'D)
      Fuck it. Give it to me.

Igor hands her the scarf. She throws it around her neck and continues walking.

EXT. WEST 10TH ST. - LATER

The crew approach the 10th St. They turn off the boardwalk and low and behold, the Escalade is in the middle of being attached to a tow truck.

              TOROS
      No! Nooooo!

Toros runs down the street. Garnik tries to keep up. Toros starts screaming at the TOW TRUCK DRIVER that is elevating the front of the Escalade.

              TOROS (CONT'D)
      That's my fucking car. No! Detach
      it now!

              TOW TRUCK DRIVER
      Can't man. Policy. Once it's
      attached, it's coming with me.

Toros shoves the driver away from the controls.

              TOROS
      Coming with you my ass. You're not
      taking my car. Garnik! Igor! Help
      me. We'e fucked if he takes this.
      Garnik starts arguing with the
      driver as well.

                    TOROS (CONT'D)
          This isn't legal. You can't do
          this!

                    ANI
               (to Igor)
          I don't think your boss understands
          the definition of legal.

                    TOW TRUCK DRIVER
          Hey man. Don't make me call the
          police.

Ani and Igor stand on the curb watching this incident go
down.

                    TOROS
          How much?

                    TOW TRUCK DRIVER
          They'll tell you at the yard.

                    TOROS
          No, how much you want. Here. Here.
          Take it.

Toros holds out a $100 bill.

                    TOW TRUCK DRIVER
          I can't take that.

                    TOROS
          Ok, fuck you then.

Toros runs around the other side of the Escalade and jumps in
it. Turns it on, throws it into reverse and hits on the gas.

Nobody can believe what's happening. Suddenly it becomes a
tug of war between the Escalade and the tow truck. Toros is
burning rubber on the rear tires. The tow truck driver is
screaming for him to stop.

The Escalade is overpowering the tow truck and the truck's
front end starts to lift off the ground. Toros is in battle
mode.

                    TOROS (CONT'D)
          You asked for this! You're not
          taking my car.

Igor and Ani are impressed.

The Escalade's front hits the ground and tears off the attachment, taking some of the front bumper with it. The front of the tow truck slams to the ground. Boom!

Toros opens the door because lowering the window would take too much time.

                    TOROS (CONT'D)
          C'mon! Get in the fucking car! Get
          in!

Garnik, Igor and Ani run to the Escalade and jump in. Toros throws it into Drive. He swerves over the sidewalk, hits a trash can and back on to the street. He tears down 12th St.

INT. ESCALADE - CONTINUOUS

They fly under the subway tracks. Toros checks the rear view. He starts to laugh in triumph.

                    TOROS
          Nothing is going to stop me! I'm
          going to find Ivan if it kills one
          of us.

They fly up onto the Belt Parkway.

EXT. BELT PARKWAY - DUSK

We watch them traveling laterally next to the Escalade.

                    TOROS
          We are going to find this fucker if
          it takes all fucking night.

He speeds off into the last moments of the sunset.

I/E. BRIGHTON BEACH RESTAURANTS - NIGHT

The next section plays out as a montage as the crew scours Brighton Beach, Coney Island and Sheepshead Bay for Ivan.

The crew hits restaurants (Varenichnaya, Ocean View, etc.), bars (Volna, Cafe Max, etc.) with interesting interactions with staff and regulars as they ask if anyone has seen Ivan. Toros shows the Insta photo to everybody. No luck.

INT. TOROS' ESCALADE - NIGHT

They are driving to the next location. Igor touches Ani's coat.

                    IGOR
          This is real mink, isn't it?

                    ANI
          No.

                    IGOR
          Oh, it feels real.

                    ANI
          It's fucking real, asshole. But
          it's not mink. It's fucking sable.
          Worth a lot more than mink. And
          don't fucking touch it again.

I/E. BRIGHTON BEACH - NIGHT

The crew hits all the major Russian restaurants bothering people while they're eating. One manager tells them that Ivan ate there an hour ago. Toros gets hopeful.

INT. RUSSIAN BATH HOUSE - NIGHT

The crew enter and show the photo to the customers. No luck.

                    TOROS
          Where else would he be?

After a long beat...

                    ANI
          He likes gaming.

OMITTED

OMITTED

OMITTED

EXT. BRIGHTON BEACH/CONEY ISLAND - NIGHT

They continue the search. They hit an internet cafe first. No luck.

97.

Barely functioning, Garnik waits in the car as the Toros, Ani and Igor explore more establishments including a billiards hall.

INT. ESCALADE - NIGHT

They continue the hunt. Suddenly out of nowhere, Garnik vomits. He then cups his mouth and continues to vomit, causing it to spray.

                TOROS
    No!!!!

                             HARD CUT TO:

WIDE EXTERIOR.

Toros slams on the brakes. The cars behind the escalade slam on their brakes. Blaring horns and screaming obscenities. Toros pulls to the side of the road. Garnik is wallowing in pain. Igor and Ani are both amused and disgusted.

                                   CUT TO:

EXT. BROOKLYN GAS STATION - NIGHT

Garnik leans on the car as Toros cleans the interior.

                TOROS
    What did you give him, goddamn it!

                IGOR
    (Russian)
    He vomited because he has a
    concussion, not because of
    Oxycodone.

Toros notices Ani and Igor are having a smoke right next to the gas pump.

                TOROS
    Honestly... with how this day has
    been going... get the fuck outta
    here!

They walk away from the pumps. Igor attempts small talk but mostly it is silent and awkward. They snub out their smoke.

INT. ESCALADE - NIGHT

Toros is fuming, Garnik is holding his head, looking quite sick.

Ani and Igor are exhausted.

          TOROS
Clubs should be opening now. Which ones did you go to with him?

          ANI
I don't know. We hit a bunch.

          TOROS
Take me to every one.

EXT. BRIGHTON BEACH - VARIOUS CLUBS - NIGHT

The search continues. Toros shoves his bright phone in people's faces. He shows the photos to managers, bouncers and bartenders.

          TOROS
See this guy? Has he been here tonight?

          BOUNCER
Yeah, he was here. We cut him off about an hour ago.

This happens at every bar/club they hit. It seems they are just missing Ivan, sometimes by minutes. They are one step behind him.

          IGOR
          (Russian)
He's doing a crawl. He's on a bender.

Ultimately no luck. It's been a long night. Everyone looks like shit. Garnik has gotten higher and higher as the hours pass.

          CUT TO:

INT. DINER - BROOKLYN - NIGHT

It's very late. The crew is seated at a booth. Garnik is inebriated. Ani and Igor are tired and hungry. Toros is on the verge of tears.

TOROS
I'm so fucked. I'm so fucked. We have six hours to find him and get to City Hall.

Toros takes a beat.

TOROS (CONT'D)
Ivan fucked me harder than he fucked you, trust me.

Ani's in no mood to argue.

ANI
Oh yeah?

Igor disagrees but keeps it to himself.

GARNIK
If we haven't found him by now, we're not finding him.

TOROS
Did I ask you? Keep your opinions to yourself.

ANI
Give me one of those oxy's.

IGOR
No.

ANI
Why?

IGOR
Because I don't have anymore plus I don't deal drugs.

ANI
(mocking his accent)
'Cause I don't deal drugs.

IGOR
I don't.

ANI
Yeah right, a gopnik who can afford to live at Brightwater and not deal drugs, ok?

IGOR
I'm a gopnik? (beat) I'm living with my grandmother.

100.

                    ANI
          Pfft. Faggot ass bitch.

Igor is sightly taken aback.

                    IGOR
          Why am I faggot ass bitch.

                    ANI
          They say you're born that way. I
          don't know.

The table behind them is getting especially rowdy. They are
clubbers having their end of the night drunk food. It's
driving Toros crazy. Finally, Toros stands and addresses the
clubbers.

                                        CUT TO:

INT. HEADQUARTERS - MAIN ROOM - NIGHT

The camera moves up the hallway of HQ. We reveal that it is
Ivan, clearly very drunk and wearing sunglasses. He walks
down the long hallway toward the main room. A red neon HQ
sign hangs above a victorian couch at the entrance of the
room. Diamond and JENNY (21) smile and say hello to Ivan as
he passes. Diamond recognizes him and looks at Jenny.

                                        CUT TO:

INT. DINER - NIGHT

Toros is standing up lecturing the table of clubbers.

                    TOROS
          Your entire generation are entitled
          babies, you know that?
          It's disgusting. Look at you. No
          respect for elders or authority. No
          ambition. No goals. Except to buy
          your new cool sneakers.

                                        CUT TO:

INT. HEADQUARTERS - LOCKER ROOM - NIGHT

Lulu and two other dancers are in the locker room. Diamond
excitedly enters. She slams her Strawberry Yoo-hoo down on
the make-up table.

                    DIAMOND
          Ani's fucking billionaire husband
          just strolled in and he's looking
          for action.

                    LULU
          Vanya?

Diamond chucks her bills in her money box and sprays herself
with perfume.

                    DIAMOND
          And I'm going to give him some.

She takes a swig of mouthwash and spits it.

                    LULU
          Vanya's here?

                    DIAMOND
          'Scuse!

Diamond pushes past Lulu and turns back to her.

                    DIAMOND (CONT'D)
          That marriage must be in the toilet
          already.

                                                  CUT TO:

INT. DINER - NIGHT

                    TOROS
          No work ethic. Lazy. Stupid.
          Arrogant. Uneducated. Tik Tok all
          day. Instagram. Spoiled. What is
          wrong with you? I've been working
          since 16-years-old.

The clubbers laugh at this Karen moment.

                    ANI
          He's at HQ!!!

The guys spin and look at Ani who is reading the text on her
phone.

                    TOROS
          Where?

                    ANI
          Fucking HEADQUARTERS!

INT. HEADQUARTERS - NIGHT

Ivan, already drunk, is at the first floor bar. Two girls flanked him as he does a few shots. Diamond approaches from behind and shoves her way next to Ivan.

INT. HEADQUARTERS - NIGHT

Diamond is grinding hard into Ivan's lap.

          DIAMOND
  You're Vanya, right?

A big smile on Ivan's face.

          IVAN
  That's me.

                        HARD CUT TO:

EXT. DINER - NIGHT

The group is marching across the parking lot to the ESCALADE.

          ANI
  Got ketchup on my fuckin' sable.

          TOROS
  Go. Go. Get in! Get in the fucking
  car!

                        CUT TO:

INT. TOROS' ESCALADE - NIGHT

          ANI
  Still stinks, bro.

They tear out of the parking lot and race to HEADQUARTERS.

EXT. BQE - NIGHT

The Escalade races through the night.

                        CUT TO:

INT. HEADQUARTERS - PRIVATE ROOM - NIGHT

The dirty lap dance continues as Ivan slams down hundreds.

                    DIAMOND
          Why don't we go upstairs to a
          private room?

                                             CUT TO:

EXT. BROOKLYN BATTERY TUNNEL - NIGHT

The gang drives through the tunnel.

                                             CUT TO:

EXT. HEADQUARTERS - NIGHT

The crew arrives and jumps out of the Escalade. They race inside.

INT. HEADQUARTERS - NIGHT

The crew walks down the long hallway.

                    ANI
          Where is he?

                    LULU
          Don't flip but he's upstairs in a
          private with Diamond.

                    TOROS
          Oh thank god!

Ani has no words. She storms across the floor, the crew right behind her. They pass numerous dancer/client interactions. Some dancers recognize Ani and call her name.

They walk swiftly up the stairs and down the other hallway, through the 2nd floor main room and in the back area where the private rooms are.

There are multiple rooms and almost every door is shut.

                    ANI
          Vanya!

                    TOROS
          IVAN!

INT. HEADQUARTERS PRIVATE ROOM - CONTINUOUS

Diamond and Ivan immediately halt the humpin'. Ivan puts his finger to his lips and makes the "shhhh!" sound.

                    TOROS
    Fuck it!

Toros opens one of the doors. Wrong room. Ani and Igor follow suit. Garnik is too slow to take action.

                    SOMEONE IN ROOM (O.S.)
    'What the hell!'

Lots of wrong rooms and pissed off dancers and clients. Some naughty things happening behind some of those doors. Finally...

Ani opens the door to the right room. They storm in. Diamond jumps off Ivan.

                    ANI
    Get out!

Ivan starts to get up.

                    TOROS
    Not you! Sit down!

Diamond moves out of the way of Ani and the crew surrounding Ivan.

Lots of drama.

                    ANI
    Ivan!

                    TOROS
      (Russian)
    You son of a bitch!

                    GARNIK
    Look! Look at my face. This is your
    fault!

Ivan is drunk and does not want to deal with any of this. He puts his hands in the air as if he is surrendering.

                    IVAN
    Ok. Ok. Ok.

                    ANI
    Ivan. Look at me. What's going on?

                    IVAN
          Hello.

                    ANI
          Ivan. I've been calling and
          texting. Why didn't you...Why
          didn't you wait for me. I was
          coming but they forced me to stay.
          They tied me up and fucking gagged
          me.

Ivan laughs.

                    ANI (CONT'D)
          It's not a joke Vanya. They
          assaulted me and... we've been
          looking for you all night Vanya!

                    IVAN
          I'm found.

                    ANI
          Please talk to them. They think
          we're going to get divorced.

                    TOROS
          It's not a divorce because it's not
          a marriage, it's an annulment.

Ivan doesn't answer.

                    ANI
          Ivan!

Ivan still doesn't reply.

                    ANI (CONT'D)
          IVAN!

                    IVAN
              (Russian)
          Stop screaming. That's fucking
          loud. Shit.

                    ANI
          Tell them you don't want this.

                    IVAN
              (Russian)
          Are my parents here yet?

                    TOROS
               (Russian)
          They'll be here at noon. C'mon!
          We're getting this annulled.

                    ANI
          Wait. Shut up. I said I wanted to
          talk to him. Hold on! Ivan, what
          the fuck. We're married. Let's stay
          married. Ivan.

Ivan looks at Toros and back to Ani.

                    IVAN
               (Russian)
          What do you want me to do? There's
          nothing I can do.

                    ANI
          What? What do you mean? I... I... I
          want to stay married to Ivan. Don't
          you?

                    IVAN
               (Russian)
          Do we have to talk about this now?

                    ANI
          Yes! Ivan! Yes! Right now!
               (to Toros)
          This isn't fair. He's drunk. He
          doesn't know what's going on.

Diamond stands in the doorway with a big smile.

                    DIAMOND
          And we just dropped some molly.

                    ANI
          Fuck off! Can you get her the fuck
          out of here...

Garnik tends to Diamond and starts pushing her away from the
private room doorway.

                    DIAMOND
          Oh look at you? Looking for some
          company?

                    GARNIK
          Not now honey.

Dawn storms in.

                    DAWN
          What's going on? What's happening?

Lulu and Igor try to de-escalate and Diamond is all about
escalating.

Other dancers have gathered outside the private room, curious
to see what the commotion is about.

                    ANI
          Ivan... please. Talk to me. Please.

                    IVAN
              (Russian)
          C'mon. I can't handle this right
          now.

                    ANI
          And I can? Ivan. This is fucked up.

                    TOROS
          C'mon, you can talk in the car.

                    ANI
          Fuck you! He has not agreed to
          this! This is not happening!

                    TOROS
          Fuck this.

Toros pushes Ani aside and leans down to Ivan, close.

                    TOROS (CONT'D)
              (Russian)
          Ivan, your parents are going to
          disown you if you don't right this
          wrong. Your mother was crying when
          they called me. Crying! You made
          your mother cry. That is shameful.

                    ANI
          Oh what the fuck.

                    TOROS
          We are getting this sham marriage
          annulled. We are meeting your
          parents and they are taking you
          home. And you are finally growing
          up. Ok?

                    ANI
          Don't listen to him.

                    IVAN
          I have to go back to Russia.

                    ANI
          Ok, and I can come with you.
          Whatever you're going through with
          your family, I'm here for you
          because I'm your wife.

                    IVAN
          That's not a good idea.

                    ANI
          No, if I have to live there until
          we sort things out, that's what
          we'll have to do. Because we're in
          this together, right?

                    IVAN
          Maybe this whole thing wasn't such
          a great idea.

Ani doesn't know if Ivan is serious but she knows there is truth in that statement.

                    ANI
          What wasn't?

                    TOROS
          Ok, let's go.

Ivan stands.

                    ANI
          Ok? Ok? Just like that?

                    TOROS
          Yes, let's go.

INT. HEADQUARTERS - KITCHEN - CONTINUOUS

Jenny walks swiftly through the kitchen and down the hall. She leans in to the office.

INT. HEADQUARTERS - OFFICE - CONTINUOUS

Jenny leans into the office.

                    JENNY
          Jimmy! Ani's out there with three
          goons causing a scene.

                    JIMMY
          Russian Ani?

INT. HEADQUARTERS - PRIVATE ROOM / THROUGH CLUB - CONTINUOUS

Toros grabs Ivan by the collar and drags him out.

                    TOROS
               (Russian)
          Run and I'll sic him on you.

Ani can't just leave like this.

                    ANI
          Wait. Ivan. I love you and you love
          me. Right?

Toros points to Igor.

                    TOROS
               (Russian)
          And trust me, you don't want that.
               (English)
          You do this to your family... and
          me... and then just go on a bender?
          Disgraceful.

They exit the room and begin walking out of the club. Diamond trails behind them throwing insults at Ani.

                    DIAMOND
          This is crazy funny. You in here
          braggin', all proud... playing high
          and mighty like your shit don't
          stink. Look at you now bitch.

The crew led by Toros is escorting drunk Ivan out of the club. Jimmy and run down the stairs.

INT. HEADQUARTERS - STAIRS - CONTINUOUS

Ani follows followed by Igor and Garnik. They make it down the stairs. Diamond is stalking them hard, pushing past Garnik.

                    DIAMOND
          And guess what bitch... he told me
          he was going back to Russia
          tomorrow and he just wanted one
          last bang!

If Ani is fazed by this, it doesn't show.

                    GARNIK
          Don't fuck with her.

Garnik points to his broken nose. Diamond doesn't back down.

                    DIAMOND
          Come back here again without these
          fucks and you won't be leaving.

Igor tries to diffuse the situation.

                    IGOR
          Ok, ok.

INT. HEADQUARTERS - MAIN FLOOR / FRONT ENTRANCE - CONTINUOUS

Ani continues to march ahead. They make it on to the main floor... almost to the front entrance. Jimmy and Dawn are trailing.

                    DIAMOND
          And looks like I called it, don't
          it?

Ani slows down.

                    DIAMOND (CONT'D)
          Two weeks on the fucking nose.

Ani turns and... explodes. She swings and charges Diamond. Igor tries to intercept but Ani is too fast. Ani tackles Diamond and their bodies hit the floor. Toros holds on to Ivan for dear life. Everybody tries to stop the fight making the moment even more chaotic. Full on brawl. Igor, Garnik, Jimmy, Dawn and a security guard are doing their best to stop it. Some girls are coming to Diamond's defense while Lulu and others defend Ani. Punches and kicks. A table is pushed over, glasses shattering on the floor.

In the back lap dance area, three topless dances including Sunny react to the noise.

Back on the floor...

                    JIMMY
          Cut it! Eddie! Cut it!

The music stops... now just the sounds of screaming and swearing. Jimmy has had enough of this drama in his club.

                    JIMMY (CONT'D)
          Out of here now! I don't care if
          you take it outside but get out of
          here.

Finally Igor pulls the kicking and screaming Ani off Diamond and drags her out the door.

EXT. HEADQUARTERS - 552 W. 38TH ST. - NIGHT

They load into the Escalade. Toros shoves Ivan in the back between Garnik and Igor. He turns and shoves the Ani in front.

INT. ESCALADE - NIGHT - CONTINUOUS

                    TOROS
          We got you, we got you, we got you.

Ani, still trying to calm herself down, turns and tries to talk sense in to Ivan to no avail.

                    ANI
          Vanya! You have to listen to me
          right now. They are trying to get
          us divorced. Do you understand what
          is happening?

No response from Ivan.

                    ANI (CONT'D)
          Pull over. Ivan and I aren't
          finished talking.

                    TOROS
          You can talk at the courthouse.

                    ANI
          That wasn't the deal.

                    TOROS
          The deal is that you get 10K and
          walk away and that's what's
          happening.

                    ANI
          Vanya! Do you hear him? They want
          me to take money to leave you!

No answer.

                    ANI (CONT'D)
          Vanya!

                    GARMIK
          Oh my god. Will someone shut her
          up.

                    ANI
          Vanya!

                    IGOR
          He's passed out. He doesn't hear
          you.

                    ANI
          This wasn't the deal. Vanya doesn't
          know what's happening.

                    TOROS
          Yes he does. He knows he fucked up.
          He knows he's going back to Russia.
          We wouldn't have had to chase him
          all night if he didn't know that.

                    ANI
          He's scared.

                    TOROS
          Yes! He should be. And when the
          judge asks him if he wants an
          annulment, he'll say yes... because
          if he doesn't, his father cuts him
          off.

                    ANI
          You motherfucker. This isn't fair.

                    TOROS
          Life isn't fair.

Ani screams in frustration and pounds the dashboard. Igor
leans forward, around the right of the headrest.

                    GARNIK
          Can we go home now?

                    TOROS
          No, we're staying here in
          Manhattan.

Ani is silent, calculating her next move, while they drive
through the city. Toros continues to chastise Ivan.

TOROS (CONT'D)
You really must hate me. Really.
And that is sad to me. Because I
let you get away with so much shit
over the years. Bailed you out
countless times. But I thought you
finally grew up.

EXT. COURTHOUSE - CENTER STREET - NIGHT

The Escalade parks in front. Toros throws it into park and settles back.

TOROS
Now we wait.

Ani looks lost as she stares out the window. Igor is aware of Ani's state.

EXT. COURTHOUSE - CENTER STREET - MORNING

TOROS
Ok, c'mon. Wake up. There he is.

Ani is wide awake. Igor and Garnik begin to stir. Ivan doesn't.

TOROS (CONT'D)
Ok, c'mon. Wake up. There he is.
Let's go!

Toros gets out of the Escalade. Ani turns to Ivan who is still quite intoxicated.

ANI
Don't worry, I'm going to handle this.

EXT. COURTHOUSE - DAY

Toros is shoving Garnik in the front seat of the Escalade.

TOROS
Do not get a ticket, do not get
towed, do not fall asleep. Keep
your phone on. Hear me?

Toros motions for the crew to walk up the steps of the courthouse where MICHAEL SHARNOV (late 40's), the NYC family lawyer greets them.

                   SHARNOV
Good morning everyone. Ok, the judge is being very kind and bumped us up... Hello Ivan.

Ivan doesn't acknowledge.

                SHARNOV (CONT'D)
       (Russian)
Ivan. It's Michael Sharnov, your father's attorney. Remember me?

                    TOROS
He's tired.

                   SHARNOV
I see.
       (to Ani)
And you are...

                     ANI
The lucky lady.

                   SHARNOV
I see. And who is this?

Sharnov points to Igor.

                    TOROS
We may need him.

                   SHARNOV
Ok, not sure what that means and don't want to know. Let's go. Get your ID's ready.

INT. COURTHOUSE - ROTUNDA - DAY

They look like quite the motley crew as they walk through the rotunda.

                   SHARNOV
       (Russian)
I talked to him. I know he wants this done. But does he know that his son is inebriated?

                    TOROS
          (Russian)
     He's not inebriated. He just woke
     up.

                    SHARNOV
     Toros please. C'mon man. I can't
     risk losing my license...

                    TOROS
     I repeat... do you want to continue
     working for the Zakharov family, or
     not?

                    SHARNOV
     Why do I agree to this shit. C'mon.

INT. COURTHOUSE - COURTROOM - LATER

The crew walks in to the courtroom and settles in front of
the judge's bench.

                    JUDGE
     Ok Mr. Sharnov. Consider yourself
     fortunate our schedule is on the
     lighter end today. Now, what's the
     urgent matter.

                    SHARNOV
     Your honor, we are here to file a
     complaint and request for immediate
     annulment of a union that took
     place under duress. Ivan Zakharov
     and...

Sharnov looks at Ani's ID.

     ...Anora Mikheyova married on...

He looks at the marriage license.

     ...January 10th...

                    ANI
     Duress my fucking ass.

Gasps and from the entire courtroom. The judge hits his gavel
several times.

116.

JUDGE
First and last warning. I hear profanity again and you'll all be charged with disorderly conduct. Mr. Sharnov, what's going on?

SHARNOV
Your honor...

ANI
This is bullshit. My husband and I do not agree to this annulment. It is being forced upon us...

TOROS
Shut up! She does agree. Get her out of here.

The room blows up.

ANI
Me and my husband, who is clearly intoxicated and unable to make an informed decision, are being forced by these men to annul our legitimate marriage.

TOROS
She's drunk and doesn't know what she's saying.

JUDGE
Ok, order in the court.

ANI
I'm not drunk... we were legally married at a legitimate marriage center in Las Vegas and have the license to prove it. Neither me nor my husband will be signing anything.

Sharnov does a double take.

SHARNOV
They got married in Nevada?

He looks down at the license and sees the State of Nevada seal.

TOROS
Yeah, so?

                    SHARNOV
          Um, you didn't tell me that.

                    TOROS
          So?

                    JUDGE
          Mr. Sharnov, you and your clients
          will be escorted from this
          courtroom...

                    SHARNOV
          Yes, your honor. No problem. Just a
          second your honor.

Sharnov turns to Toros again and speaks to Toros in Russian.

                    SHARNOV (CONT'D)
                (Russian)
          I can't get it annulled here.

                    TOROS
                (Russian)
          What are you talking about? Why?

                    SHARNOV
                (Russian)
          They got married in Nevada. This is
          New York.

                    TOROS
          Yeah and?

                    SHARNOV
                (Russian)
          We can file for one but if you want
          this now, you have to go there.

                    TOROS
          Are you fucking kidding me?

                    SHARNOV
          We need to... I need... I'm
          requesting...

                    JUDGE
          Out of my courtroom now!

Thee courtroom is chaos.

                                              CUT TO:

OMITTED

EXT. COURTHOUSE - STEPS - DAY

On the front steps, the freaking out continues. Toros makes a scene.

                    TOROS
          Why the fuck did you get married in
          Vegas? Couldn't you have gotten
          married here?

                    ANI
          We were in Vegas when we decided
          to. When Ivan fucking proposed to
          me!

                    TOROS
          I'm so fucked. I'm so fucked.
          They're landing in two hours. My
          heart. I honestly think I'm going
          to have a heart attack.

Toros sits down on the steps of the courthouse. He holds his head and weeps.

EXT. TORO'S ESCALADE - DAY

Toros opens the front door and tears Garnik out of the front seat.

                    GARNIK
          All done?

                    TOROS
          No! They fucking got married in
          Vegas.

                    GARNIK
          What?

The crew piles in and Toros drives away.

INT. TOROS' ESCALADE - DAY

They drive in silence. Toros wiping tears from his eyes. Ani, again seated in front.

Suddenly Ivan starts vomiting on himself. Igor and Garnik start to freak out. Toros barely reacts.

                    TOROS
               (Russian)
          I don't care. Shit yourself for all
          I care. I don't care anymore.

They all lower their windows. Ani doesn't know what to think.

                                             CUT TO:

EXT. PRIVATE AIRPORT - DAY

The Escalade drives on to the property and parks in front of
the hanger entrance.

OMITTED

EXT. PRIVATE AIRPORT - TARMAC - DAY

The Zakharov private jet lands. Toros walks onto the tarmac
to greet them. They are walking down the boarding stairs. Two
customs agents approach with a customs sniffer dog.

                    TOROS
               (Russian)
          Hello Nikolai Zakharov. Hello
          Galina Stepanovna.

                    GALINA
               (Russian)
          Where is he?

                    TOROS
               (Russian)
          He's inside.

The dog sniffs Galina as she b-lines it for the terminal.

Toros turns to Nikolai who is lighting a cigarette.

                    TOROS (CONT'D)
               (Russian)
          So I have some bad news.

                    NIKOLAI
               (Russian)
          More bad news?

                    TOROS
          Yeah.
               (beat)
          You're not going to be happy...

NIKOLAI
(Russian)
I'm already not happy.

Toros does not want to say it.

TOROS
Well...

NIKOLAI
Well what?
(Russian)
The hooker's a guy or something?

TOROS
(Russian)
No. No. But they didn't get married here in New York. So we can't get an expedited annulment.

NIKOLAI
(Russian)
Oh my god. Where did they get married?

TOROS
Vegas.

NIKOLAI
(Russian)
Of course he did. Little bastard.

INT. PRIVATE AIRPORT - TERMINAL - DAY

Galina storms in. Garnik, Igor and Ani stand.

GALINA
(Russian)
Ivan, is this true? What did you do? You smell like alcohol.

Ivan holds his head in his hands. Vomit stains all down the front of his jacket.

GALINA (CONT'D)
(Russian)
He's drunk? Garnik, he's drunk!

GARNIK
(Russian)
Yes, ma'am. He's intoxicated. Not our fault.

Ani slowly approaches Ivan and Galina.

      IVAN
    (Russian)
  Mom! Stop! This is embarrassing.

      GALINA
    (Russian)
  Disgusting! You're embarrassed? Do
  you know how embarrassed your
  father and I are! You've disgraced
  us.

      ANI
    (Russian)
  Hello Mrs. Zakharov, I'm Anora.
  It's so wonderful to finally meet
  you. I'm so grateful to be Ivan's
  wife and a part of your beautiful
  family.

Galina turns to Ani.

      GALINA
    (English)
  Ivan is not your husband and you
  are not part of this family and
  your Russian is embarrassing.

Ani remains composed.

      ANI
  M'am, Vanya and I are in love and
  we would like you to accept this
  marriage.

      GALINA
  Vanya is not in love with you. And
  we will not accept this.

Ani looks at Ivan who looks away. Ani almost vomits.
Suddenly, Toros and Nikolai enter the terminal.

      NIKOLAI
    (Russian)
  Galina! Galina! Um... Toros has
  something to tell you.

EXT. PRIVATE AIRPORT - TARMAC - DAY

Galina, dragging Ivan, is leading the crew through the hanger
toward the plane at a swift pace. Ani is numb and walking
with them. Igor stays close.

                    GALINA
              (English)
          Fuck! You are all idiots. How could
          this happen!

                    ANI
          Vanya.

Ivan doesn't look back.

                    ANI (CONT'D)
          Vanya.

                    GALINA
          Shut her up. And Toros, we will be
          discussing your future of lack of
          one with the company. You let him
          trot off to Vegas, my god. Hurry!

They see the assistants bringing luggage off the plane.

                    GALINA (CONT'D)
              (Russian)
          No, back on the plane!
              (to Toros)
          I want us refueled and in the air
          in 10 minutes! Fuck!

                    TOROS
              (Russian)
          Yes, Ma'am.

Galina, Nikolai, Toros and Garnik board the plane. Ani stops at the bottom of the steps.

                    ANI
          Vanya!

Ivan finally turns around.

                    IVAN
          What!

                    ANI
          So we're just going to get
          divorced!?!

                    IVAN
          Yes! Of course! What are you
          stupid?

Ani doesn't know what to say. Ivan's demeanor shifts.

                    IVAN (CONT'D)
          But I want to thank you for making
          my last days in America fun.

Ani has given up the fight.

                    ANI
          Yeah, you had fun?

                    IVAN
          Yes, now let's go.

Ani does not follow. She watches Ivan ascend the steps. She turns away. Igor who is waiting next to her, averts his eyes.

INT. PLANE - CONTINUOUS

Ivan boards the plane and takes his seat.

                    GALINA
          Where is she?

OMITTED

OMITTED

EXT. TARMAC - MOMENTS LATER

Galina swiftly descends the steps.

                    GALINA
          Board the plane now.

                    ANI
          I'm not doing that.

                    GALINA
          You're getting on that plane and
          getting a divorce.

                    ANI
          Oh, I'll be getting a divorce.
          Sure. But I'm getting a lawyer,
          suing Ivan and your family and I'll
          walk away with half. We don't have
          a pre-nup.

Long beat.

GALINA
          Do that and you lose everything.
          Any money you may have, although I
          doubt you have any, will be gone.
          You have a house? A car? All
          gone.(she leans in) Your life and
          the lives of your family and
          friends will be destroyed. If you
          doubt I can do that, please go
          ahead, see what happens.

INT. GULFSTREAM G650 - DAY

They are mid-flight. The interior of the plane is lavish and
gaudy. There are two seating areas, a food and drink area and
a couch facing a wide screen TV. Russian news plays on the
TV.

Ivan and his parents are seated on one side of the plane. Ani
and Igor are seated on the couch in the rear. Toros sits
across from Garnik on the other side.

It's been a long night and the crew is looking spent.

                    IGOR
          Netflix and chill?

                    ANI
          Fuck no.

In the front, Ivan's parents will not let up from
reprimanding him. He tries to defend himself but he spirals
into drunken nonsense.

Toros tries to interject at some point, which only causes
tensions to flare.

Igor stares at the bar. He goes over and pours two shots of
vodka. He returns and hands her one. She takes it. Igor lifts
his glass to toast. Too late, Ani does the shot. She turns to
see him holding the shot glass in the air.

                    ANI (CONT'D)
          Like I would have toasted you.
          Pfft.

On the other side of the plane...

Garnik, drink in hand, leans over to the family...

                    GARNIK
               (Russian)
          I just want to say that it is an
          honor to be finally able to spend
          time with your wonderful family and
          thank you so much for trusting in
          Toros and I over the years...

The family dismisses him in disgust.

                    TOROS
          Shut up. Why are you drinking?
               (under his breath)
          You fuckin' idiot.

Toros takes the drink out of his hand.

                    TOROS (CONT'D)
          You know what? Go. Go back there.
          Go.

Garnik stumbles to the back.

He plants himself on the couch next to Ani and Igor.

                    GARNIK
          I understand and forgive you for
          what you did.

                    ANI
          Ok great. I'm so grateful for your
          forgiveness.

Garnik lays his head down on the couch and is asleep in seconds.

Igor and Ani have a back and forth that is aggressive, yet has a playful undercurrent.

In the front of the plane, the argument has reached its peak. Ivan is crying.

                    IVAN
               (Russian)
          I'm sorry, ok! God. Look, She was
          my escort for the week and we got
          drunk and got married. Sorry! But
          we're going to fix it so come on,
          stop. Jesus.

This is too much for Ani to bear. She stands and gestures toward Ivan on the other side of the plane.

                    ANI
              (Russian)
          I'm glad to be divorcing your sorry
          ass. You're pathetic, man.

                    TOROS
          Igor.

Igor pulls her to sit back down on the couch.

                    ANI
          Pathetic bitch ass motherfucker.

Ani is boiling inside. After a beat...

                    IGOR
          What's your favorite color?

                    ANI
          My favorite color?

Ani tries to read Igor.

                    ANI (CONT'D)
          The fuck? Why?

Still reading...

                    IGOR
          I don't know. Just a question.

                    ANI
          Are you macking on me right now?

                    IGOR
          Macking?

                    ANI
          You find this the opportune time to
          mack on my ass right now?

                    IGOR
          What's macking?

                    ANI
          Why?

                    IGOR
          Why what?

                    ANI
          Why do you want to know?

                    IGOR
          Because I don't know what else to
          talk about and we're sitting next
          to each other for the next three
          hours.

                    ANI
          Fuckin' scumbag, man. Now? Pffft.
          And asking my favorite color?
          That's like junior high school
          level macking. Fucking Russian
          girls must be easy, shit.

Now Igor gets it.

                    IGOR
          I was actually asking to take your
          mind off him. And I should add...
          you're not my type. I wasn't
          macking.

Ani stares and reads him.

                    ANI
          Lie.

                    IGOR
          Not a lie.

                    ANI
          Liar.

                    IGOR
          No.

The plane lands in Las Vegas.

EXT. AIRPORT - LAS VEGAS - LATE MORNING

The group gets in two black SUVs on the tarmac.

I/E. SUV - DAY

They drive through Las Vegas.

EXT. RAPID DIVORCE CENTER - PARKING LOT - DAY

They pull in and park in front of a rapid divorce center.

INT. RAPID DIVORCE CENTER - DAY

Everybody piles into the small office. The receptionist is taken aback by the amount of people. The ATTORNEY greets them and starts the annulment process.

Garnik is asleep on a chair in the corner.

Ivan does not think twice when asked to sign the papers.

Ani is disgusted. She steps forward.

          IGOR
     (Russian, interjecting)
So, I don't want to be out of line but I think it would be appropriate if Ivan apologizes to Anora.

Toros cringes.

          GALINA
     (Russian)
Actually, that is out of line. My son won't apologize to anyone.

          TOROS
     (Russian)
It's okay, look, he doesn't know what he's talking about. He's tired, y'know, he's helped us all day.

          ANI
Because your son's a pussy.

Toros turns his attention to Ani and starts to escort her out.

          GALINA
And you are a disgusting hooker.

          ANI
And your son hates you so much that he married one to piss you off. Your family is trash.

Ani looks at Ivan.

          ANI (CONT'D)
Take a last look 'cause this is the best you'll ever get, bitch.

Toros immediately escorts Ani and Igor out.

                    GALINA
          Wait, is that my scarf?

Ani looks down at the scarf and slowly slides it off her neck
in a taunting way. She drops it to the floor. Toros reaches
down and picks it up for Galina as Ani and Igor exit the
room. Ani then takes off her Sable and throws it on Ivan's
head. She then exits.

EXT. RAPID DIVORCE CENTER - DAY

Ani takes the designer sunglasses out of her coat and puts
them on.

Toros walks them to one of the SUVs. As Ani and Igor get in
the SUV, Toros gives instructions to the driver and hands
Igor key car and bank card.

                    TOROS
          Take them to Harry Reid, domestic
          flights.

He looks to the backseat.

                    TOROS (CONT'D)
          Igor is going to take you back. You
          can stay at the house tonight but
          you need to be out in the morning.
          Igor will get your money when the
          bank opens.

Beat.

                    TOROS (CONT'D)
          And thank you.

Toros goes back into the divorce center.

I/E. SUV - DAY

Ani and Igor drive through Las Vegas to the airport. It's a
silent ride.

INT. COMMERCIAL AIRPLANE - DAY

Ani and Igor are on a crammed domestic flight. Ani is asleep.
A baby cries. Igor covers Ani with his jacket.

                    CAPTAIN
          Flight attendants please prepare
          for landing.

EXT. LAGUARDIA AIRPORT - CURB - DUSK

They take a taxi from the airport. The sun is setting.

INT. MANSION - MASTER BATHROOM - NIGHT

Ani takes a shower. When she is drying off, she looks around the gorgeous bathroom. Nice while it lasted.

CUT TO:

INT. MANSION - LIVINGROOM - NIGHT

Ani is smoking a blunt. Igor is on the couch aside her. They are not speaking. New York 1 plays on the TV. The weather report is covering the snow storm about to hit the tri-state area. Finally Ani passes Igor the blunt. He accepts.

              IGOR
Happy Birthday to me.

              ANI
It's your birthday?

              IGOR
Yesterday.

              ANI
Yesterday was your birthday?

              IGOR
Yeah.

              ANI
Happy Fucking Birthday.

              IGOR
Thank you. (beat) I was 30.

              ANI
Great.

              IGOR
I like Anora.

Ani turns and looks at him with a "WTF" face.

            IGOR (CONT'D)
The name. Anora.
                (beat)
The name. More than Ani.

She turns back to face forward.

                    ANI
          Says the fuck head named Igor.
               (beat)
          Fucking... Igor.

                    IGOR
          Igor means warrior. It's a good
          name.

                    ANI
          Yeah? Igor means hunchback weirdo
          you, fucking clown. Can you shut
          the fuck up, please?

                    IGOR
          Toush.

                    ANI
          What?

                    IGOR
          Toush.

                    ANI
          Touché? You fucking moron?

                    IGOR
          Touché.

                    ANI
          Try figuring out English before
          attempting French you, dumb fuck.

                    IGOR
          And your name is better?

                    ANI
          Fuck no. That's why I don't fuckin'
          use it.

                    IGOR
          But what does it mean?

                    ANI
          What does what mean?

                    IGOR
          Anora.

                    ANI
          In America, we don't care what
          names mean. And I'm not interested
          in conversation, man.

Igor googles it.

A few moments of silence as they light up cigarettes.

                    IGOR
          You're better off this way, trust
          me. This is a fucked up family.

                    ANI
          Did I ask for your fucking opinion?

                    IGOR
          No.

                    ANI
          Exactly.

                    IGOR
          Ok, I was just being nice.

                    ANI
          Nice? You fucking assaulted me,
          dude. So go fuck yourself.

                    IGOR
          I didn't assault you.

                    ANI
          You don't call that assault? You're
          right... it's fucking BATTERY... as
          well as fuckin' kidnapping and I'm
          sure a million other felonies. Fuck
          you, dude.

                    IGOR
               (Russian)
          That wasn't assault. I had to calm
          you down. You didn't get hurt.

                    ANI
          What? You attacked me, tied me up,
          gagged me. You're psychotic.

                    IGOR
          You were in no danger of injury or
          harm.

ANI
Pffff. If Garnik wasn't there,
you'da raped me, guaranteed.

IGOR
I would have raped you?

ANI
No doubt.

Ani gets up off the couch, walks to the fridge to grab a VOSS water and begins walking toward the stairs.

IGOR
Why would I have raped you?

ANI
I can see it. You sick motherfucker
would've raped me. You have rape
eyes.

IGOR
I have rape eyes?

ANI
Yes.

IGOR
No. I wouldn't have raped you.

Ani turns.

ANI
Oh yeah... why?

IGOR
Why?

ANI
Yeah.

IGOR
Why what?

ANI
Why wouldn't you have raped me?

Igor thinks about it for a moment.

IGOR
Because... I'm not a rapist?

134.

                    ANI
          Nope, because you're a faggot ass
          bitch.

She turns towards the stairs. Igor has nothing. He watches her ascend. He sits there for a moment and then grabs the remote and turns off the TV. He hears Ani's footsteps on the stairs.

Ani comes back down the stairs with a pillow. She throws a pillow on the couch.

                    IGOR
          Goodnight.

                                              CUT TO:

INT. MANSION - MASTER BEDROOM - NEXT MORNING

Ani lies in bed after she wakes. It's snowing and she looks out to a winter wonderland.

                                              CUT TO:

Ani is packing. Clothes, photo frames, toiletries.

INT. MANSION - LIVINGROOM - LATER

Igor slowly awakens on the couch. He sees the falling snow.

INT. MANSION - FOYER/DOORWAY - LATER

Ani and Igor are leaving the mansion, wheeling out her three large pieces of luggage. They open the door.

It's snowing.

                                              CUT TO:

EXT. BANK - DAY - LATER

It continues to snow outside. We see Igor and Ani making the transfer with a bank teller.

                                              CUT TO:

                    ANI
          Nope, because you're a faggot ass
          bitch.

She turns towards the stairs. Igor has nothing. He watches her ascend. He sits there for a moment and then grabs the remote and turns off the TV. He hears Ani's footsteps on the stairs.

Ani comes back down the stairs with a pillow. She throws a pillow on the couch.

                    IGOR
          Goodnight.

                                                  CUT TO:

INT. MANSION - MASTER BEDROOM - NEXT MORNING

Ani lies in bed after she wakes. It's snowing and she looks out to a winter wonderland.

                                                  CUT TO:

Ani is packing. Clothes, photo frames, toiletries.

INT. MANSION - LIVINGROOM - LATER

Igor slowly awakens on the couch. He sees the falling snow.

INT. MANSION - FOYER/DOORWAY - LATER

Ani and Igor are leaving the mansion, wheeling out her three large pieces of luggage. They open the door.

It's snowing.

                                                  CUT TO:

EXT. BANK - DAY - LATER

It continues to snow outside. We see Igor and Ani making the transfer with a bank teller.

                                                  CUT TO:

                    ANI
          Pffff. If Garnik wasn't there,
          you'da raped me, guaranteed.

                    IGOR
          I would have raped you?

                    ANI
          No doubt.

Ani gets up off the couch, walks to the fridge to grab a VOSS
water and begins walking toward the stairs.

                    IGOR
          Why would I have raped you?

                    ANI
          I can see it. You sick motherfucker
          would've raped me. You have rape
          eyes.

                    IGOR
          I have rape eyes?

                    ANI
          Yes.

                    IGOR
          No. I wouldn't have raped you.

Ani turns.

                    ANI
          Oh yeah... why?

                    IGOR
          Why?

                    ANI
          Yeah.

                    IGOR
          Why what?

                    ANI
          Why wouldn't you have raped me?

Igor thinks about it for a moment.

                    IGOR
          Because... I'm not a rapist?

EXT. ANI'S APARTMENT/INT. IGOR'S CAR - DAY

Igor and Ani are parked in front of Ani's apartment. The snow is coming down hard.

Igor reaches into his pocket and pulls out the ring and passes it to her (the one she cut his face with).

                    IGOR
          Don't tell Toros.

Ani takes it.

                    ANI
          Thank you.

Ani places it in her inside pocket. He jumps out and grabs the luggage and brings it up to the porch. He notices Ani has not exited the car. He comes back to the car and opens the door and looks in.

                    IGOR
          Ok?

                    ANI
          Have a cigarette?

Igor gets back into the car. He reaches into his inside pocket and gets a pack. He gives her a cigarette and takes one for himself. He lights both. They sit in silence and smoke. The only noise is the steady windshield wiper.

                    ANI (CONT'D)
          This car is very you.

                    IGOR
          It's my grandmother's.
              (beat)
          You like?

                    ANI
          No.

They finish the cigarette. They both chuck their butts through the crack in their windows.

Ani stares at Igor. It's awkward. Finally she moves toward him. He's not sure how to react. She climbs on top of him, forcing the seat back.

                    IGOR
          What are you doing?

Ani reaches down, opens his pants and takes off her panties. Igor is slightly resisting but finally relents. She quickly gets him aroused and sits down on him and rides him. He is confused and concerned yet allows it to happen.

Suddenly she explodes and begins punching and slapping his face. He is completely taken by surprise. Ani lands a shot or two as he scrambles to block her pounding fists. Ani screams as she pounds away. Finally Igor gets hold of her hands and subdues her. He holds her wrists so she cannot continue swinging.

                      IGOR (CONT'D)
          (Russian)
Stop! Stop! Just fucking stop! What is wrong with you!

Ani begins to sob and collapses on him. He holds her as she cries.

EXT. ANI'S APARTMENT/BROOKLYN STREET - DAY

The snow continues to fall around the idling car.

                                                            CUT TO:

CREDITS.

Made in the USA
Las Vegas, NV
05 March 2025